MARK TWAIN'S JEWS

Also by Dan Vogel

The Three Masks of American Tragedy

Emma Lazarus

MARK TWAIN'S JEWS

by

Dan Vogel

KTAV Publishing House, Inc.
Jersey City, N.J.

Library of Congress Cataloging-in-Publication Data

Vogel, Dan.
  Mark Twain's Jews / by Dan Vogel.
      p. cm.
  Includes bibliographical references and index.
  ISBN 0-88125-916-0
  1. Twain, Mark, 1835-1910 – Political and social views. 2. Jews in literature.
  3. Antisemitism in literature. I. Title.
  PS1342.J48V64 2006
  818'.409 – dc22

                        2005032946

                        Published by
              KTAV Publishing House, Inc.
                    930 Newark Avenue
                   Jersey City, NJ 07306
                      bernie@ktav.com
                      www.ktav.com
                   Tel. (201) 963-9524
                   Fax. (201) 963-0102

Typeset by Jerusalem Typesetting, www.jerusalemtype.com
Cover Design by Jan M. Phair

For
My Sisters,
Lillian Brickman נ"י
and
Mildred Smitman ע"ה

ACKNOWLEDGMENTS

I MUST ACKNOWLEDGE the aid of several librarians who acquired materials for me: At the Hebrew University Library in Jerusalem, Mss. Sarai Safir and Chana Schwartz. At the Mark Twain Project at University of California at Berkeley. At The Joseph Kushner Hebrew Academy, Livingston, NJ, my son, Shimon Vogel.

I must also express my gratitude to Prof. Jonathan Sarna at Brandeis University who encouraged me at the beginning of my project. It was just a brief exchange of e-mails, but encouraging nevertheless.

Dan Vogel
Jerusalem

Table of Contents

INTRODUCTION

FROM THE LATE 1850S on to the year of his death, Mark Twain (1835–1910) mentioned Jews dozens of times in notebook entries and autobiographical recollections; in newspaper articles and personal letters; in sketches and essays – occasionally hooking them somehow tangentially to the topic in hand. One reads Charles Neider's collections, *Complete Essays of Mark Twain* and *Complete Humorous Sketches and Tales,* with some surprise that the Jews received infinitely more attention than the Negro in the tumultuous pre- and post-Civil War period in which he flourished.

Though in his fiction, both novels and stories, he did not create a Jewish character until the latter years of his life, and none of his Jewish characters that he did create has even a smidgeon of the immortality of slave Jim in *Adventures of Huckleberry Finn,* the frequency of glances at the Jews in his non-fiction testifies that the Jews were forever in the front of his mind. There seems to be no biographical cause for his sustained and frequent interest in the Jews. It was not empirical. Mark Twain did experience Jewish acquaintances through his lifetime – American Jews and European Jews whom he met during his frequent travels on that continent – but he came to really know only a few of them. Nor was there any involvement with the American Jewish community until a few years before death in 1910. There is no evidence that these life experiences seemed to have caused any untoward feelings about Jews.

Mark Twain's Jews are not the Jews he met or might have found in a history of the people, or in contemporaneous characterizations he may have come across about this people that lives apart. He developed in his own mind a personal, perhaps idiosyncratic amalgam of an extraordinary race characterized by an exotic and mysterious flavor, touched with awesomeness as the only surviving biblical race – a perception kneaded, however, with unsavory ancient myths that had survived into the 19th century, and affected the growing Mark Twain since he was born Samuel Langhorne Clemens. His knowledge of this people was really an anecdotal selection from reading the Bible, popular literature of his own time, and calumnies absorbed from childhood on.

His readers did not react to the intermittent references to Jews in his essays and sketches before the publication of "Concerning the Jews," his major statement about anti-Semitism in 1899. However, since its publication, that essay has been the subject of controversy. In his own day, some Jewish readers saw it as a well-intentioned essay, but diminished by misinformation about Jewish history and character; others read it as a welcome sympathetic analysis of anti-Semitism and its amelioration. In ensuing generations, however, reading the same essay, some readers and scholars have aggrandized doubt into near-certainty that Twain was indeed not guiltless of anti-Semitism. For decades now, Mark Twain has been on trial as harboring anti-Semitic tendencies.

The debate voices viewpoints of all sorts. Some scholars pursue the normal academic endeavor of trying to know as much about an author as possible. Even here, however, scholarly objectivity seemed to demand that every writer must be condemned to undergo a period of revision of reputation, and Mark Twain has suffered a bit from some of the things he had said about the Jews. However, in my estimation, this minor, if persistent, feature of the Twain canon can have no effect upon Mark Twain's stature as a great American writer – so American and so great that Ernest Hemingway and William Faulkner, no slouches themselves, thought him to be the progenitor of true American fiction.

Other critics, like Cynthia Ozick, genetic products of centuries of periodic pogroms, larger holocausts, and painful migrations, are inevitably more sensitive to statements about Jews by the famous and influential. One feels an atmosphere of either disappointment or defense when they write about the subject. When great literary artists fall into the quagmire of anti-Semitism, it is especially painful. The presence of the despicable, ape-like Viennese Jew in T.S. Eliot's poem, for example, notwithstanding the stature of Eliot as a 20th-century cultural guru, poet, and literary theoretician, is seen as a blemish upon him, an aberration, not be veneered over by his place in the cultural world.

Controversy makes the critical world go 'round, but even so, one is surprised by the extremes of the debate surrounding Mark Twain, almost always conducted, of course, with stiff conventional courtesy. An attempt was even made in 1939 to make Twain into a Nazi, which engendered a defense of him by no less a respected academic than Bernard de Voto. In 1980s and '90s the decibels of the debate became more persistent and strident with scholars on both sides. One example is displayed in the very titles of two articles: In 1985, Sholom J. Kahn published an article blatantly entitled, "The Philo-Semitism of Mark Twain." Undeterred, however, Andrea Greenbaum countered in 1996 with an article entitled, "'A Number-One Troublemaker': Mark Twain's Anti-Semitic Discourse in Concerning the Jews." My involvement in the subject of Mark Twain's Jews was aroused by this essay and I wrote a rejoinder that was published two years later.

Writing that little remonstrance, I came to feel that Mark Twain deserved a more thorough investigation and judgment about his perception of Jews. After all, to this day, Mark Twain represents the epitome of the American dream – the perceived embodiment throughout the world of the mythic American values: humor, liberalism, tolerance, self-reliance, good sense, egalitarianism. On the Jewish side, America was always the "goldene medina" to the American Jew, whether refugee, free-willed emigrant, or native-born: the golden world of opportunity and freedom for the perennially persecuted in Europe and all other Jews. In his own day, the Jews of America practically lionized

Mark Twain. Can it be that, nevertheless, his own statements label this paragon as anti-Semitic?

Hence, this monograph. The only way to be fair in judgment of Mark Twain's remarks about Jews is to consider the evidence. First and primary are the written statements and utterances by Mark Twain himself about the Jews, as many as I could find, from his boyhood to his last moments, those that saw the light of print in his lifetime, as well as those published posthumously.

The organization of this material is generally chronological, but that is complicated: Chronology in this instance is not a matter of history or biography but of perspective. What Twain wrote in his younger days I will sometimes free from the confines of chronology in order to immediately compare or contrast with what he said in subsequent years. Sometimes Twain started a literary endeavor, dropped it for a while, then worked on it sporadically, perhaps even over years. This, too, may require anachronistic commentary. The changes he made can be quite revealing.

Along the way, I also offer remarks by family, friends, and other contemporaries, comments by scholars and critics who have studied and written about his works, and my own running commentary. All these references, contexts, and evaluations constitute my attempt to present Mark Twain's Jews as objectively as I can.

One more aspect of this study needs to be previewed here: To judge anyone as anti-Semitic requires an authoritative definition of the term. I shall synopsize recent authoritative comments about American anti-Semitism in Mark Twain's time and for all eras, that can serve as a guide to judgment by readers of this monograph as to whether Mark Twain can fairly be branded as anti-Semitic or not. Your judgment is my reward for undertaking this study.

Chapter One
"THE HANNIBAL SYNDROME"

The Town of Hannibal

In 1835, in Florida, Missouri, Samuel Langhorne Clemens was born. Sam's father, John M., had brought his family to the tiny town, foreseeing a future for it. He determined to be part of it and profit financially. He became a merchant, then a member of a county development commission, and finally a county judge. However, apparently little Florida, Missouri, did not develop rapidly or economically enough, and in 1839, he sold most of his property there and moved to another Mississippi River town, Hannibal.[1]

In Hannibal, Mark Twain was born – of course, long before he chose this *nom-de-plume* for his sketches and stories. The seeds of the future, however, were planted in Hannibal town. Missouri in the 1840s was a state in the throes of the birth pains of the Civil War, and Hannibal, numbering a thousand residents when the Clemenses arrived, was a hotbed of bigotry. It was naturally anti-Negro and it was surprisingly anti-Jewish. There were a few Jewish families there, which, like identical families throughout the Mid- and Far West began by peddling and sought a place to strike roots in store-merchandising. One needs only to peruse the introductions to towns and cities in *A Jewish Tourist Guide to the U.S.*, by Bernard Postal and Leonard Koppman, to be struck by the frequency of the same scenario of a single Jewish family opening a store in a tiny town, prospering a bit, thereby attracting another family or two to emigrate there. There is no entry for Hannibal in the *Tourist Guide*, which indicates that whatever Jews there had been in the town in those days left no memorial of their presence.

That there had been Jews in Hannibal, however, is recorded in the local press by way of excoriating the local Jewish merchants for "sharp practices" and price-gouging.[2] There was a family named Levin or misrecorded as Lesem that owned the clothing store.[3] Mark Twain's memory sixty years later, when he dictated portions of his autobiography, conjured up two little Jewish boys named Levin, outsiders, hangers-on who ran with (or sometimes from) his gang. Twain recollected that in the Hannibal elementary school these were the first Jews he had ever seen. "It took me a good while to get over the awe of it. To my fancy they were clothed invisibly in the damp and cobwebby mold of antiquity. They carried me back to Egypt, and in imagination I moved among the Pharaohs and all the shadowy celebrities of that remote age." Perhaps this mystique so fascinated Mark Twain throughout the years that he mentions Jews infinitely more frequently than Negroes, the race that dominated attention in his time. "We had a collective name for [the Levin boys, recalled Twain] which was the only real and large witticism that was ever born on those premises. We called them Twenty-two – and even when the joke was old and had been worn threadbare we always followed it with the explanation, to make sure that it would be understood, 'Twice Levin [read: '(e)leven'] – twenty-two.'"[4]

The ground was all prepared for young Sam Clemens's imbibing anti-Semitism.[5] Into the fresh American hinterland – though it was bedeviled by its own immediate fears of a major confrontation concerning Negro slavery – probed the insidious finger of the ancient myth of "Christ-killer." The teaching in the Sunday school that young Sam Clemens attended was decidedly fundamentalist and therefore anti-Semitic. The Levin boys having made an "awful impression" on the gentile boys, Sam Clemens among them, the gang wondered, "Shall we crucify them?" Indeed, it was conjectured by the gentile boys that one town resident who had drowned had judgment thrust upon him for protecting the Levin boys "when they were being chased and stoned" by Sam and friends in vengeance for a crime that their Sunday school laid upon all Jews everywhere.[6] (The writer of this monograph remembers his boyhood days a century later in Jersey City, NJ, playing "crucifixion" with his two Polish Catholic pals – there were no other pals – in the role of the spread-eagled star.)

In his early teens Sam Clemens worked as a printer's apprentice on one of Hannibal's newspapers. In all probablity, setting the stories of price-gouging owners of the clothing satore, he subliminally absorbed the anti-Jewish content of what he saw sanctified in print. Thus, the nature of "Jewish race" was taking shape in Mark Twain's mind, and it was not positive.

Whatever else John Clemens, Sam's father, left him, it was restlessness and a burning desire to make and handle gobs of money. He also left him the bad luck to make a botch of it. Like his father, seeking his fortune in larger arenas, Sam Clemens, in the summer of 1853, age 18, left Hannibal. But Hannibal never left him, not for all the 57 years that he had yet to live.

The Syndrome

Henry Nash Smith, pre-eminent Twain scholar, called the intrinsic Hannibal influence "The Matter of Hannibal," meaning how Mark Twain used latent memories of the town for settings or atmosphere in his stories. The literary term "matter" recalls the heroic days of Greece and Rome as the subject-matter of epics and medieval poetry. Not so Hannibal. Instead of "The Matter of Hannibal," I shall use a label more appropriate to our subject as the legacy of this town: "The Hannibal Syndrome." It was a kind of disease normally in remission whose symptoms would intermittently, gratuitously, slither out of Mark Twain's subconscious to infest his writings as brief, passing slurs about the Jews as a race.

The most positive and famous use he made of Hannibal is for the idyllic "St. Petersburg" setting in *Adventures of Tom Sawyer*.[7] However, the more characteristic memory seems to have been his much-later transformation of Hannibal into the town of Eseldorf in *The Mysterious Stranger* (begun 1897, reworked later) which was despoiled by Satan himself:[8]

> Eseldorf was a paradise for us boys. We were not overmuch pestered with schooling. Mainly, we were trained to be good Christians, to revere the Virgin, the Church, and the saints above everything. Beyond these matters we were not required to know much; and in fact not allowed to.[9]

Significantly, this saintly town was precisely the place that Satan found spiritually easy to penetrate and prosecute his wily ways. Twain's last thoughts on Hannibal seem to be darkly satirical.

But not yet in 1853–56. These years found him traveling back and forth among cosmopolitan St. Louis, New York, and Philadelphia, with intermittent pauses in Keokuk, Iowa, and Cincinnati, Ohio. The social and literary air around him simply confirmed the anti-Jewish prejudices he had ingathered in Hannibal, Missouri. From Louis Harap's survey of the popular novels of this period,[10] one can imagine what young Sam Clemens, bright, curious, already a nascent writer himself, and ambitious for a place in the literary sun, would have found himself smothered under. A few examples would characterize this onslaught of financially successful best-seller fiction:

John Holt Ingraham's *Moloch, the Money-lender; or the Beautiful Jewess* (1845, "often reprinted"): The very title expresses two themes that we shall encounter in Mark Twain's later utterances and writings concerning Jews. The "Beautiful Jewess" was a conventional Lilith-like image in the contemporary fiction, but the only recorded beauteous Jewess that Mark Twain was passingly acquainted with was Adah Menken in Virginia City, Nevada, in 1864, of whom more in a later chapter. There are passing appreciative mentions of the Jewish woman, racially considered, in *Innocents Abroad* (1869), but never bewitching. Of greater importance is the mythical Jewish lust for money, embodied in the stereotypical cruel and evil usurer, like Moloch (a child-consuming fire-god in the Bible) in Ingraham's opus.

The usurer's appearance is not infrequent in these mid-19ᵗʰ-century novels, nor, obliquely, it is true, in the Twain canon. What can be expected of a young aspirant reading a novel like John Beauchamp Jones's *Western Merchant* (1849): Moses Tubal opens a store in Hannibal, Missouri (!); he is a cheat and a parasite sucking away at the Christian community. Here, no doubt for a young, dreaming writer of fiction, is confirmation of what he had experienced in Hannibal. In the same author's *Border War* (1859), the evil Jew is named "Solomon Mouser." This time Sam Clemens as Mark Twain would come to make up for this characterization – Twain's "Solomon"-named characters in his later writings are positive characters.

There is a novel of the time that one would like to think did influence Sam Clemens to cleanse his latter years' characterizations of the Jews. Joseph Scoville's *Vigor* (1864) presents "Simpson of Chatham Street," a Jewish pawnbroker and money-lender, who is "a man of integrity," deserving of a "larger percentage" of the interest he takes because "he relieves [the] pain and anguish" of his needy clients. Quite a contrast to the other contemporaneous characterizations of the Jewish businessman. Sam Clemens's conversion was not immediate. Simpson will have to wait 30 years before Mark Twain would rise to attest to the general honesty of Jewish businessmen in New York in "Concerning the Jews" (1897/9), and would resurrect Simpson as honest "Solomon Isaacs" in *The Mysterious Stranger*.

Meanwhile, back in the 1850s, Clemens's symptoms of the Hannibal Syndrome were not out-of-place among this literature. After a few months in New York (August–October 1853), he landed in Philadelphia. In a letter sent from the City of Brotherly Love in November 1853, he remarks that Jewish occupants of two historic houses "desecrated" the premises, a rather religiously-inspired verb to use. In April 1857, he wrote a piece for the Keokuk (Iowa) *Daily Post*, that contained the conventional anti-Jewish jibes that he admitted years later appeared "so often in the Hannibal newspapers of the latter 1840s." An article he wrote for a Cincinnati newspaper described how, during the terribly cruel winter of that year, the "blasted Jews" "adulterated" the fuel by mixing coal dust with ground pepper.[11] Perhaps Sam Clemens, start-up journalist in those days, was trying to please his editorial bosses, who may have edited their newspapers with the same prejudice as the editors of the Hannibal sheets.

Clearly, as Janet Smith wrote in *Mark Twain and the Damned Human Race,* "Mark Twain was not born to tolerance."[12] A number of scholars agree, but they simultaneously, and justifiably, rush to his defense. Smith herself goes on to claim, "He achieved [tolerance] and had it thrust upon him by experience. And perhaps that was why it ran somewhat deeper in him than the lip service which sometimes passes for that quality."[13] Philip Foner recognizes that Twain was indoctrinated with anti-Semitism, "yet it must be said that the stereotype of the Jew is entirely absent from Mark Twain's subsequent writings."[14] In our ensuing survey, we shall discover, lamentably, "entirely" is not entirely accurate. Shelley Fishkin, in her article on "Racial Attitudes" in the *Mark Twain Encyclopedia,* for example, avers that "Mark Twain never managed to transcend completely the limits of his time, his place, and his race," all causes of the Hannibal syndrome. Yet it must be insisted immediately that Fishkin's "Never," as we shall see, may not be entirely accurate either.

Perhaps the most balanced observation to make at this point is that Sam Clemens/Mark Twain (he adopted this pen name in 1863) may have recognized the Hannibal tendency in himself, subliminally. Having visited the Sandwich Islands (Hawaii) as a newspaper correspondent in summer 1866, he wrote an essay in 1873 about the natives he observed there. The essay contains the following statement: "Their ancient superstitions are in their blood and bones, and they keep cropping out now and then in the most natural and pardonable way"[15] "Natural" and above all "pardonable" are the key words that demand our judgment. I can think of no better description of Mark Twain's "Hannibal syndrome" than this one, which he himself wrote. Nor a more accurate prediction of how the symptoms will crop out in his own future writings.

The connection between the context of Hawaiian natives and our subject can, of course, be considered by some too tenuous to be persuasive. But very late in life, Mark Twain came back to this unwitting apologia in a context perhaps more personal, this time on a literary matter. In an essay he called "Is Shakespeare Dead?" (1909), he considered the tradition an egregious mistake that Will Shakespeare wrote what had for centuries been attributed to him. Twain's passage reads like a retrospective summation of the Hannibal Syndrome:

> I am aware that when even the brightest mind in our world has been trained up from childhood in a superstition of any kind, it will never be possible for that mind, in its maturity, to examine sincerely, dispassionately, and conscientiously any evidence or any circumstance which shall seem to cast a doubt upon the validity of that superstition. I doubt I could do it myself.[16]

But he tried mightily to do so. To what extent he was successful, is at the center of the current debate concerning his attitude to The Jew and is the centrifugal concern of this monograph.

Mark Twain visited Hannibal several times in his life, never spending more than a few days there. He enjoyed tramping the well-known streets and taking pictures with surviving buddies of the days they chased the Levin boys together. He seems to have kept in touch with a number of them, for in his *Autobiography* he knows whom he had outlived and who still walks the earth. On the other hand, Carl Dolmetsch counted 168 residents of Hannibal in Twain's late-life recollection, and in many instances he gave unflattering, even unsavory details about them.[17] Evidently he fought against the grace of nostalgia as he came to fight against the "Hannibal syndrome."

Today, Hannibal's tourist industry profits from Samuel Langhorne Clemens's sojourn there: "Mark Twain" appears in front of the supermarket, a movie house, a motel, etc. Certainly he would not have objected to making money by permitting the use of his pen name, but perhaps he would have felt that the relatively few years he spent there and what the town had taught him makes the situation (to use one of his favorite phrases) "a bit too many."

Chapter Two

OUT WEST WITH TWO JEWS
AND A RIGHTEOUS GENTILE

FOR NINE YEARS after leaving Hannibal, Sam Clemens (not yet "Mark Twain") wandered in the East and Midwest, alighting here and there for varying periods of time, like the children of Israel in the Bible. In several places he inserted a toe into journalism, lacing his feature stories, as we've noted, with Hannibal-standard anti-Jewish jibes. For four of those years he lived on the Mississippi River, first as passenger, then as a pilot. Finally, he joined his brother Orion and traveled westward, landing in Virginia City, Territory of Nevada, in August 1862. If any one moment in any man's life can be called *the* turning point of his life, this was it for Samuel Langhorne Clemens.

In 1862, Virginia City was not the clapboard-saloon-and-dust town of Western movies. It was a center of silver mining and sophisticated enough to vie with San Francisco as the cultural center of the West, with a population of educated and concerned citizenry, theater, and, above all, good newspapers.[1] It attracted a Jewish population that in 1862 formed a Bnai Brith lodge, bought a plot for a cemetery, and two years later organized a congregation. This community included significant families, like the Michelsons: Albert grew up there in the 1860s, went East for an education and eventually won the Nobel Prize in Physics in 1907; Charles, born there in 1869 became a famous journalist and Franklin Delano Roosevelt's publicity director in 1932. Ben Davidson was Rothschild's representative in the American West[2] – too bad that Sam Clemens, who always lusted for quick-money investments, did not know to take advantage of Davidson's presence. Perhaps rubbing journalistic shoulders with heads of this community whetted Sam Clemens's interest in the race that produced them.

It was here that Sam Clemens met two Jews and a righteous gentile that would mold him and concern him for years to come.

An Education in Humor

That gentile was Artemus Ward. Artemus Ward can be recognized as one of the formulating artists of Western humor as a literary and lecturing profession. His following throughout the continent was vast and appreciative. And he was a generous soul. Unafraid and unenvious of new talent, without prejudice of any kind, he became the companion and mentor of Sam Clemens. Ward had already made his mark as a humorous lecturer and graciously tutored Clemens in the art. Under his tutelage, Clemens, who adopted the literary alias "Mark Twain" in 1863 as a new jazzy *nom-de-plume* like all the Western humorists whom he befriended, developed from an amateurish, diffident personality onstage to a confident, polished, carefully rehearsed humorous lecturer.

In an affectionate recollection ten years later, "First Interview with Artemus Ward," Mark Twain relates how he received his first, perhaps most important, lesson in dead-pan humor, the style he was to adopt for much of his own non-fictional humor. On this occasion, after being introduced to the newcomer and matching swigs of whiskey, Ward assumed "a look of superhuman earnestness" and launched into a long monologue of confusing information and sequiturs about silver ore and mining and concluded with a question, "Do you not think so?" Mark Twain, profoundly confused, blamed his inability to follow what Ward had said on the whiskey. So Ward repeated the performance, "more fearfully impressive than ever," to no more success, and yet a third time with "determined impressiveness" until the "dread solemnity" was broken by laughter.[3] Thus Mark Twain, lecturer-to-be, learned with what demeanor onstage he should deliver his monologues: earnestness, impressiveness, solemnity, impervious to the latent humor.[4]

Artemus Ward's connection with Mark Twain's Jews is not in any remark or statement; rather his tutoring honed Twain's remarks and statements about them. Twain applied what he had learned from Ward in his allusions to Jews in his sketches: the tone is deceptively earnest, the sly insertions are funny, but also contain sometimes a subtle spoor of satire, nearly always without direct offense to either the audience or the Jews.[5] Further on in this monograph, we shall see that Mark Twain applied his lessons from Artemus Ward sometimes too well. Some of his jibes at Jews, written in a context of "dread solemnity" earned him, in some quarters, the accusation of being "anti-Semitic."

It would not be the first time that the technique boomeranged back to Twain. For example, in 1870, Mark Twain felt it necessary to publish two essays about the over-success of two hoaxes he had published several years earlier, in 1862 and 1863, as news features, at the time he was a companion to Artemus Ward. One was the famous "The Petrified Man," the other "The Dutch Nick Massacre." Twain was amazed that both were reprinted widely, believed unstintingly, even though he inserted many verbal clues to make sure the satirical humorous intent is communicated. He admits that it is "really hard to foist a moral or a truth upon an unsuspecting public through burlesque without entirely missing the point."[6] Twain had to undergo the dubious satisfaction of writing another essay explaining the fact that the original was a hoax; I say "dubious satisfaction," because a writer cannot be totally satisfied if his effort is not understood by his readers, even if the original intention over-succeeds. Twain learned lessons from these incidents.

Artemus Ward died at the age of 33 in 1867. For the remainder of his life, Mark Twain was to benefit from Artemus Ward's transformation of Clemens clay into Mark Twain art. In 1880 Mark remembered him as "one of the kindest and gentlest men in the world."[7] "His pseudonym," wrote Justin Kaplan, "had become his identity – Artemus Ward had swallowed up Charles Farrar Browne [his birth-name] – and this problem, along with his mantle and following, now passed on [with his death in 1867] to his friend and protege," Mark Twain, né Samuel Langhorne Clemens.[8] But at his death, Ward had left his protege, not yet fully formed, to a more dubious and suspicious mentor, Bret Harte, a 25% Jew.

Friend and Nemesis

Bret Harte's grandfather was Bernard Hart (*sic*), a wealthy, devout Jew living in New York. A formidable gentleman of business, he helped found the New York Stock Exchange in 1792. He was active in Shearith Israel, the "Spanish-Portuguese" Synagogue, until his death in 1855. Astoundingly, in 1799, he married Catherine Brett, a non-Jew, violating one of the major taboos of the Jewish religion. Why he did so can only be conjectured.[9] In any case, this union was dissolved within a year, but a son Henry was born of it. Henry, in turn, married a gentile girl of Dutch descent and fathered Bret Harte (Henry had added the "e").

Now, Bernard married a second time. This time his bride was Rebecca Seixes, daughter of a prominent Sephardi (Spanish/Portuguese) family in colonial and revolutionary America, deeply connected also to Shearith Israel. With her he produced a number of children of pure Jewish stock. Their knowledge of their connection with the famous writer, Bret Harte, is not at all clear. Helen Davis, who thoroughly investigated Harte's ancestry, at one point asserts that none of Bernard Hart's "Hebrew" descendants knew of his earlier union,[10] but at another point she writes that Bret Harte's daughter (that is, the granddaughter of Henry, the son of Bernard's first, non-Jewish wife) said that "her father never made a secret, in the home circle, of the fact that he had a Jewish grandfather."[11] Apparently, the fact that "Bret Harte was one-fourth Jewish"[12] was known also to his friends in the West in the 1860s, including Mark Twain, but Western tolerance merely absorbed the fact. This survey of Bret Harte's ancestry, and the synopsis of his relationship with Twain that follows, will give us the context in which to consider presently the only reference Twain makes about Harte as a Jew.

They met in San Francisco in 1864. Harte was already far ahead of Mark Twain in the literary profession and in journalism, as well. Twain watched, fascinated and intimidated, as Harte prepared the first issue of the *Overland Monthly,* which in quality came to rival the high-class eastern magazines. Two years later, after publishing sketches in the *Virginia City Territorial Enterprise, San Francisco Call, New York Mercury,* and elsewhere, Mark was delighted and overwhelmed when Harte proposed a joint collection of sketches. Though the project fell through, he savored the invitation because he saw Bret Harte "'at the head of my breed of scribblers in this part of the country'"[13]

In February 1867, Twain offered a miscellany of his own to Artemus Ward's publisher, and was rejected, but the publisher did take on a miscellany by Harte. Twain was too busy to brood over this development: he was offering his miscellany to other publishers and he had signed on to travel with the aristocratic tourists on the *Quaker City* to Europe and the Middle East and write letters back to the San Francisco *Alta California* and a couple of New York newspapers. On his return, the publishing house run by Elisha Bliss would invite him to write a book based on these letters.

Meanwhile, Mark Twain had hit continent-wide exposure in May 1867, for his miscellany *The Celebrated Jumping Frog of Calaveras County and other Sketches.* James Russell Lowell thought that the title story, told in the serio-comic, laid-back, laconic style that Bret Harte wrote in, was "the finest piece of humorous writing ever produced in America." Harte might well have intuited that this was a harbinger of rivalry for his lordship of the genre, which is perhaps why the future relationship between him and Twain was frequently rocky.

Harte read the manuscript of *Innocents Abroad,* and, like Artemus Ward before him, offered Mark Twain advice. He told him which chapters to leave out (and published them separately in the *Overland Monthly*) and what lapses of style to rewrite. "It was a kind of thing for Harte to do," Twain recalled later, "and I think I appreciated it." His continued warmth for Harte can be felt in the comment that "The Luck of Roaring Camp" (1868) is "Bret's very best sketch and most finished – is nearly blameless."[14]

However, the warmth didn't last. A serious falling-out centered upon Harte's review of *The Innocents Abroad*. For some reason, Harte could not get a copy when he wanted it and wrote Mark Twain an apparently virulent letter about it, described by Mark as *"the most contemptuous and insulting letter you ever read"* (Twain's emphasis).[15] Now, *The Innocents Abroad* was written by a Western writer as a humorous travel book, but Harte's review in the January 1870 *Overland Monthly* was, in Justin Kaplan's judgment, "laced with literary condescension and cosmopolitan fastidiousness," more in the nature of a picayune Eastern elitist reviewer than one in a Western magazine.[16] It was also treacherous, since Harte had read the manuscript before publication, and made suggestions which Mark Twain followed. Harte evidently had not commented on these offending characteristics when he had read Twain's original manuscript. Perhaps he now felt more keenly that Mark Twain was becoming the rising rival star of Western-inspired literature, and *Innocents Abroad* would push him to the zenith. Their friendship at this moment, says Kaplan, fell to "absolute zero."[17]

And yet, the irony is that Twain persisted in extolling Harte as the head of the pack. In a letter of March 1871, he called Harte the "most celebrated man in America today" as a result of "The Heathen Chinee" poem that swept the American continent. Harte's star, Twain felt, eclipsed him.[18] An accusation that Mark Twain plagiarized Bret Harte stung Twain sharply enough to elicit the following statement in a letter to Thomas Bailey Aldrich (January 28, 1871):

> I did hate to be accused of plagiarizing Bret Harte, who trimmed and trained and schooled me patiently until he changed me from an awkward utterer of coarse grotesquenesses to a writer of paragraphs and chapters that have found a certain favor in the eyes of even some of the decentest people in the land .

In the same paragraph, he laments, "Bret broke our long friendship a year ago without any cause or provocation that I am aware of."[19]

But 1872 found Bret Harte as a house guest in the Clemens

household in Hartford, Conn. (Sam had married Olivia Langdon in February of '70), borrowing his host's money and drinking his host's whiskey. Of such frequency was he that Mr. Clemens, in a municipal census, straight-facedly listed "F. Bret Harte" as a boarder.[20] The disenchantment was growing, however, because Harte made no attempt to pay back the substantial loans Mark gave him. As far as the whiskey is concerned, Twain was amazed one night when Bret Harte, with a deadline for a promised story on the morrow, went to his room drunk and spent the rest of the night writing what his host considered one his best stories, "Thankful Blossom."[21] (This long story about a triangular love affair during the Revolutionary War lacks the frontier characterizations, humor, and bite of Harte's famous tales. It is hackwork. To my thinking, Twain's judgment was clouded by his amazement that Harte could write a coherent story at all in his alcoholic condition.)

There were business fallouts, too. They were both now writers for Elisha Bliss's publishing house, where Mark Twain was a stockholder. He had "pleaded" with Harte to give his *Gilbert Conroy* to Bliss, who was preparing the publication of *Tom Sawyer*. But Bliss was delaying everything, as selling season upon selling season slipped past. Finally in September 1876, Harte wrote to Twain: "…Bliss must confess he runs his concern in *your* interest, and that he uses the names of other authors to keep that fact from the public…" Mark Twain's "feelings for Harte were by now permanently poisoned," Kaplan concludes.[22]

Not quite. The two writers now entered into an ill-fated collaboration of a comedy culled from Harte's "Heathen Chinee" poem and Twain's *Roughing It*. It was entitled (perhaps fittingly) *Ah Sin*. It failed miserably in 1877, in Washington, DC, and in New York City. Nevertheless, Mark Twain offered Bret Harte $25 a week to live in Hartford and collaborate on another play. Harte, this once showing good judgment, declined.

To this point, though opportunities were rife, Mark Twain never had referred to Harte as a Jew. This is especially noteworthy: when seething over the substantial amount of loans he passed on to Harte no matter how unsavory the circumstances, he never connected Harte's financial greed to the myth of Jewish lust for money .

By 1878, Mark Twain had had it with Bret Harte. He was obsessed with tearing him down at every opportunity, not heeding his wife's warning that the public is turning against *him* for meal-mouthing an author whom they still venerated.[24] When he heard that the United States government appointed Bret Harte as a consul in a German commercial town, the inner boiling erupted. He wrote a hot letter about the appointment to William Dean Howells, his good friend who edited *The Atlantic Monthly* and was an admired novelist in his own right. In the letter Twain castigated the American government for appointing such a low character as its representative, a man guilty of the following bill of indictments:

> Harte is a liar, a thief, a swindler [a California editor had publicly accused Harte of pocketing money meant for contributors], a snob, a sot, a sponge, a coward. brim full of treachery, and he conceals his Jewish birth as carefully as if he considered it a disgrace. (Written from Heidelberg, Germany, June 27, 1878)[25]

Our purpose here is not to determine the extent of the accuracy of Mark Twain's complaints.[26] Rather, it is to exegete his statement in terms of his overall perspective of the Jewish race:

> 1. Mark Twain knew Bret Harte was "Jewish," probably since early days together in California, without caring, I imagine, what percentage of Jewish blood ran in his veins. It would seem from the litany of negative traits in this letter that Harte's care-lessness about the ethics of money may now have raised the level a bit of his Jewishness in Twain's estimation of him.

> 2. In his letter, Mark Twain, who knew something about literary strategy, saved the last indictment until it is the climactic salvo in this barrage of Harte's failings. For our purposes, it makes no difference if it is true or not that Harte hid his Jewish origins; what matters is that Twain believed that it is the worst of his crimes. From which we learn that to Twain being Jewish is no reason

for shame or concealment. The true disgrace is trying to hide it. Apparently, Twain forgot or ignored the fact that Harte did take up verbal cudgels on behalf of a Jew: he was stirred to respond to the infamous refusal of the Grand Hotel in Saratoga Springs, NY, to admit Joseph Seligman, the eminent financier, as a guest because he was "an Israelite." Harte wrote a bitingly satirical poem on the incident, "That Ebrew Jew" (1877).[27] In any case, far from any anti-Semitic tendency that would cause him to belabor Bret Harte for this accident of his birth, Mark Twain berates him for not being proud of it, or, at least, accepting it without prejudice. In Mark Twain here, there appears to be no prejudice at all – the opposite appears to be the truth.

3. Harte's Jewishness had no effect upon Twain's admiration for him as an editor and a writer, no effect on his desire to collaborate, even after the pain of a first failure. His disaffection with Harte grew, I think, with Harte's sin of never paying back the money he borrowed from Twain who, as we shall see, worshipped the acquisition of it.

4. More subliminal than that, I suggest, is Mark Twain's loss of an inner battle against envy and the fear that Harte's persistent popularity darkens his own chance of a prominent place in the sun of literary success and popularity. In this letter, he relieved himself somewhat of the weight of jealousy.

As American literary history records, Harte's meteor burnt out, Mark Twain's comet still glows across the heavens. Hamlin Garland visited the two of them in 1899. He was struck by the physical aging of Mark Twain, but equally impressed with his vigor, and had to listen to a diatribe against his alleged enemies. Twain still had enough spunk left to write memorable sketches and stories, like "The Man that Corrupted Hadleyburg" and *The Mysterious Stranger*. Garland found Bret Harte to be old, haggard, ill. He had left the U.S. forever in 1878, his best work, Garland felt, was already behind him. He still published hackwork, but was "tired and sick."[28]

Harte died in 1902. Mark Twain's vindictiveness never abated. In the essay entitled "Is Shakespeare Dead?" (1909), he exemplified the realistic though poetical quality of the dialogue in Shakespeare's plays by comparing it with the dialogue in Bret Harte's stories: "Whenever Bret Harte introduces that industry [quartz or surface mining], the first time one of his miner's opens his mouth I recognize from his phrasing that Harte got the phrasing by listening…not by experience."[29]

Bret Harte is not forgotten in the American West, and sometimes is even hyphenated with Mark Twain, whom he at first nurtured. There's a Bret Harte Street in Reno, Nevada[30] In San Francisco, where the two first met, the Bohemian Club, founded by a French Jew, Raphael Weill, adorned its facade with a bronze relief memorializing Bret Harte. In the State Exposition Building in Los Angeles hangs a large map of the counties mentioned in Harte's stories. Finally, the two are once again united, in a "Twain-Harte" summer resort in Tuolomne County, California.[31] Neither, I imagine, would be terribly pleased.

Fast Friend

Back in 1861, a Jewish individual named Joseph Goodman became part owner of a moribund newspaper in Virginia City, Nevada Territory, called *The Territorial Enterprise,* and turned it into a journal that rivaled the San Francisco papers.[32]

Mark Twain recalled in *Roughing It* that in those years his pockets were empty and he was desperate for income: "I do not doubt that if at that time, I had been offered a salary to translate the Talmud from the original Hebrew, I would have accepted – albeit with diffidence and some misgivings – and thrown as much variety into it as I could for the money." Why, of all possibilities, did Mark Twain choose the Talmud for this piece of gratuitous humor? One does not need to emphasize that Sam Clemens knew nothing of the Talmud,[33] except that it was esoteric (how esoteric, since it was written mainly in Aramaic, not Hebrew, he certainly did not know). But he did respect it – he does admit to "diffidence" in the face of the task. Yet, characteristically, he couldn't forego the last, rather inappropriate (what classic work of any people has more variety than the Talmud?), if humorous, clause.

A salary did come to be offered to him. One day in 1862 he received a letter from Mr. Joseph Goodman inviting him to become city editor of his paper, in Twain's estimation "the chief paper of the territory." Joseph Goodman hired Sam Clemens. This Jew from the early years of Nevada compensated somewhat for the roller-coaster disillusionments with Bret Harte.

A year later, 1863, Goodman became sole owner of the *Enterprise,* and a boon companion of Sam Clemens, who in that year became "MARK TWAIN." Goodman also took on the role of serving as another mentor, along with Artemus Ward and Bret Harte, of the budding humorist/novelist. He also became his fast friend, from afar and near, until Twain died in 1910. Goodman died seven years later. It never occurred to Mark Twain to ever mention that his fast friend was Jewish. It was not that that made him special.

An interesting anecdote concerns Goodman's and Twain's connection with the Jewish actress Adah Isaacs Menken (1835–1868) in the years they roiled around Virginia City. She was quite a personality. She was not born Jewish, "but was converted to Judaism…. by the mother [!] of her first husband, Isaac Menken" (the only Jew among her four spouses), an irregular conversion to Judaism if there ever was one.[34] Her conversion was nevertheless a sincere one. She took a "militant pride in her Jewishness," led a protest in 1857 in London against the exclusion of Jews from the House of Commons, never performed on Yom Kippur, even slept with a Bible under her pillow.[35] A poetess of sorts, she published poems based on biblical themes, and with Penina Moise (1797–1880) and Emma Lazarus (1849–1887) formed a triumvirate of American Jewish poetesses in the 19th century. She certainly was well-known as a Jewess when she arrived in Virginia City in 1862.

Adah Menken was not lauded for her acting, but for her notoriety. She introduced pink tights as stage-wear and the impression of nudity, as expected, caused a sensation in New York, London and the Continent. Men were automatically entranced by her, several notable ones were able to fulfill their fantasies. The cultural aspiration and financial reputation of Virginia City, though obviously provincial alongside the capitals of Europe, were evidently high enough to attract famous performers. Menken gave performances there of her famous vehicle *Mazeppa,* "clad only in pink tights,"[36] a spectacle that no doubt shocked the miners of the Comstock lode enough to crawl out of their mines and abandon their card games.

"Among her ardent suitors," reports Postal and Koppman, were Joe Goodman and Samuel Clemens." This may be an overeager statement. One Twain scholar contends that Miss Menken tried to draw Mark Twain into her crowd, "but failed to impress him favorably."[37] If true, it could not be because she was Jewish: in *The Innocents Abroad* and elsewhere, Mark Twain shows a favorable bias about the physique and deportment of Jewish ladies. Perhaps Adah Menken inspired him to pay attention to that regard in his travels.

It is significant to note that Twain's see-saw relations with Bret Harte did not prejudice him against Joseph Goodman. After Far Western free-thinking, Mark Twain evidently did not see Harte, for all his shady character, as a representative of the Jewish race. In 1871, a year after Mark Twain and Olivia married, Goodman came east to visit the newlyweds in Connecticut. He was "dumbfounded" to observe his irreverent drinking companion in Virginia City, his ex-biting-humorist on *The Enterprise,* saying Grace at the table.[38] Goodman stayed on for awhile, "filling the role vacated by Bret Harte and soon to be filled by [William Dean] Howells" as personal critic. He read and commented upon the manuscript of *Roughing It.*[39] Though Goodman was slightly younger than Twain, he served as an example of "courage, integrity, good judgment, and stability."[40]

Goodman's continual interest and concern was manifested several years later when Mark Twain published *The Prince and the Pauper,* a story of Tudor England, of all topics. "What could have sent you groping among the driftwood of the Deluge for a topic?" he asked him, and advised him to get back to what he should be writing about.[41] Who knows but that Goodman's criticism chased Mark Twain back to finishing and publishing *Huckleberry Finn* and *Life on the Mississippi* in the next three years. Regardless of the persistent popularity of *The Prince and the Pauper* (still being reprinted and adapted for television), Mark Twain's reputation and stature in American and world literature are based on the masterpieces set in 19ᵗʰ-century America, not post-medieval England. Goodman was still a keen editor.

Mark Twain last saw him in 1906 and wrote a last letter to him a month before he died in 1910. Nor is their relationship forgotten in Virginia City. On the *Territorial Enterprise* building is a plaque quite different from the type that the town of Hannibal glares in the eyes of tourists. It says simply that

> *Mark Twain Who Greatly Enriched the Literature of the West*
> *Started his Career as a Writer in this Building in 1862 on the Editorial*
> *Staff of "The Territorial Enterprise"* [42]

It is a pity that the tribute does not also declare that it was under the aegis, let us not forget, of its great Jewish editor, Joseph Goodman.

Chapter Three

"ISAAC" THE TERRIBLE

B Y THE END OF 1866, Mark Twain had absorbed all the West could do for him and he decided to climb the ladder of his literary destiny in New York. He embarked on the *America* in San Francisco to sail down to Nicaragua, cross that Isthmus, board the *San Francisco,* and sail up the east coast of the continent to the Big City. The voyage was awful. Terrible storms hit the *Columbia* on the Pacific and cholera swept the *San Francisco* as it sailed north from Nicaragua; there were eight deaths and burials at sea. All this was duly noted by Mark Twain because he had a contract to write travel letters back to the *Alta California* in San Francisco. His notes upon which his letters were based included incidents and activities on board, and descriptions and characterizations of the passengers. Two were destined to be metamorphosed into future writings.

Wakeman and Solomon

On the voyage out of San Francisco, Mark Twain met Capt. Ned Wakeman, whom he described as large, powerful, covered with tattoos, boisterous, irreverent, and teller of tall anecdotes.[1] Just Mark Twain's type of man. An anecdote Wakeman told was about an incident in the Sandwich (Hawaiian) Islands:[2] Once, preparing to sail on a brand new brig, Wakeman noticed rats "cantering" ashore one after another until none was left on board. Thereupon, he ordered his trunks to be set ashore. He was accosted, Wakeman relates, by "Solomon the Jew – what did I say his d—d name was?", who asked him why he is putting baggage on shore. In answer, Wakeman told him about sailing on a leaky, old tub, one time, that was nearly "foundering," but the boat made it nevertheless to its destination, "becus [*sic*] there were rats on board," whereas a new brig sailing the same route without a rat on board never did make it. Solomon readily deduced that the rats on the new brig presciently knew of the new ship's fate and scrambled ashore. Wakeman reported laconically, "Solomon says, 'Boy take that other trunk [presumably his] ashore, too.'" (*Alta California,* February 9, 1867)

Forty years later, both these characters will be resurrected by Mark Twain in an early version of "Extract From Captain Stormfield's Visit to Heaven" (publ. 1909). Capt. Stormfield himself originated in Capt. Ned Wakeman, and the "Solomon" of the anecdote reappears as "Solomon Goldstein," with a thoroughly sympathetic characterization, sailing together with the captain through ethereal heavens. "Solomon" had a further resurrection in the late *The Mysterious Stranger*" as "Solomon Isaacs," who turns out to be the most trusted inhabitant of the village of Eseldorf.

Enter "Isaac the Israelite"

The Jew on board the *America* in 1867 was not so fortunate in Twain's characterization. In Twain's *Notebook #7,* he is referred to only as "the Jew"; in the *Alta California* letters, he is named "Isaac, the Israelite" (February 24, 1867 issue), a mildly pejorative racial appellation. In this letter, he is merely mentioned. Characterization comes later, in the letters published on February 27 (dated December 20) and March 15 (dated Christmas).[3] "Isaac" receives a sub-heading and a long paragraph for himself in the December 20th letter. Twain describes him as "broad-shouldered and kinky-haired," and "He has been his natural self from the beginning. His vanity, impudence, obsequiousness and utter imperviousness to insult trench upon the wonderful." To illustrate this characterization, Twain reports that Isaac intrudes himself where he is not welcome – at table for meals and games, and pushing on sea-sick passengers "bad foreign sausage, good-tasting Limberg cheese, with a death-dealing smell, and execrable Dutch herring – all of which conduct looks kind and considerate – it really does but it certainly must mean business."[4]

"Isaac the Israelite" is the protagonist of two incidents that appall the passengers. The first concerns an attempt at alleged bribery: the Jew had been placed in a tiny, lower-deck cabin, and he persistently tried to bribe his way to a better location and cabin by offering the ship's captain a probably "bogus" meerschaum pipe. Consistently refused, persistence finally paid off apparently, for Isaac was relocated to better quarters.

The second incident is reported under the headline, "The Fall of the Isaac."

He had been soliciting sympathy by displaying the jewelry of his recently dead wife. Now he organized a raffle as a means to get rid of the baubles, "for it grieved him to the heart to have these momentos…of happy days." The raffle realized $350. All was satisfactory until the passengers realized that Isaac had also bought raffle vouchers and won all the better pieces of jewelry and left the other hopefuls with worthless "pinch beck." Now they doubted that he ever had a wife who died and the whole plot was "shameful."[5]

The obliteration of any sympathy or trust was complete. When Isaac prevailed upon the captain to remove a young German girl from steerage where she was "subject to insult," the passengers believed that in reality the Jew had "rascally designs against her" of his own. But Isaac got his come-uppance: They adulterated his tea and his whiskey until he had to spend all his time in his cabin "disgorging." And Twain's notes quote a set of cruel satirical verses synopsizing these adventures with "the Jew," including this stanza:

All that the stranger lacks in nose
(Repeat 2 times)
He neatly makes up in cheek.[6]

It is worthwhile to note for future reference that Mark Twain himself makes no allusion in his physical description of Isaac to his nose. It is the anonymous maker of the satirical verse who raised up the popular infamous feature prevalent in anti-Jewish diatribes and cartoons to this very day. Twain didn't attach it to Isaac here because, as the ditty admits, he didn't have one. Mark Twain will have somewhat to do with Jewish noses a bit later in his career, but not yet. At this point, it is sufficient to give him credit that he did not send the ditty on to the *Alta California* for publication. It remained buried in his notes until scholars unearthed it.

Thus, Mark Twain was to an extent selective in what he sent to the *Alta California*. Perhaps this is indicative of the most important point to make in evaluating these letters: Mark Twain's attitude concerning Jews in these years was ambivalent. On the negative side, he regurgitates obliquely shards of inherited myths residual in him since Hannibal days. Obsession with money, the myth insists, is the root of the evil of the Jew (although one day Mark Twain will insist that this is a world-wide obsession). A display of Isaac's solicitude is taken as really a business ploy. Paying for a favor is seen in a Jew as something nefarious. Residual Hannibal attitudes can be detected, I think, also in the fact that, in his notes, Twain names the other passengers he talks about, but he refers to the unsavory Jewish passenger only racially as "the Jew." In the *Alta California*, Twain gave him a coldly depersonalized name.

For all of that, Mark Twain does interpolate a sympathetic note into his account of Isaac's downfall. He was disgusted with the passengers' preening after their success in bringing Isaac down. He remarks, "They do say that when a man starts down hill, everybody is ready to help him with a kick."[7] In this statement, this Jew is somewhat individuated as a normal human.

In sum, the assertion by Louis Harap that, "It is clear that by 1864 Mark Twain was no longer carelessly making invidious references to Jews"[8] is not entirely borne out, either in Twain's accounts of this trip in 1867 (nor, we shall presently see, on the later trip to Europe and the Middle East). On the other hand, nowhere is there any iota of personal, deeply felt animosity to a Jew or Jews. The punishment meted out to Isaac is reported with the same sly asides that characterize the instances of deadpan style of Mark Twain humor in his other writings. The tone of his observations about Isaac's activities does not indicate he would have written differently about an Irishman who employed anti-social behavior. All in all, his personal notes and public letters in the *Alta California* on this occasion served as a rehearsal for what will become a major technique in the account of his travels in *The Innocents Abroad.*

Chapter Four

THE NOT-SO-INNOCENT ABROAD

Mark twain arrived in New York in January 1867. The San Francisco–New York voyage and successful letters to the *Alta California* prepared the technique that he was about to use in the letters he contracted to write about the trip to Europe and the Middle East on the *Quaker City*: select as a clique several interesting and amiable passengers who would make good copy, observe the other passengers with a humorously raised eye-brow, and slip in asides now and again veneered with soft cynicism. It worked. *The Innocents Abroad,* a revision of 50 or so letters of the dozens he dispatched back to the *Alta California,* has never gone out-of-print.

The *Quaker City* sailed on June 10, 1867. Concerning ethnic groups, Mark Twain is essentially ecumenical in his observations on this trip. There happened to be no Jews among the passengers on board the *Quaker City,* nor does he mention Jews in the Azores, the first port-of-call. The way he describes that part of the population he calls "Catholic Portuguese" lives anticipates his treatment of all groups:

> The donkeys and the men, women, and children of a family, all
> eat and sleep in the same room, and are unclean, are ravaged by
> vermin, and are truly happy. The people lie, and cheat the stranger,

and are desperately ignorant, and have hardly any reverence for their dead.[1]

The point is that Mark Twain, practicing journalist, is recording what he sees. It is not that this Christian Protestant from the American Middle and Far West is anti-Catholic.[2] We will find Twain saying pretty much the same things about other groups, including Jews, that he will observe at the ports-of-call and cities and sites along the way to Palestine, and in the Holy Land as well. In Gibraltar, for example, the Moorish merchants from Fez are turbaned, sashed, and trousered; and the "Mohammedan vagabonds from Tetouan and Tangier, some brown, some yellow, and some as black as virgin ink" are "long-robed, bare-legged [and] ragged". (No reason is given for calling them vagabonds – probably because they do not look like Americans). In Gibraltar he found "Jews from all around [North Africa], in gabardine, skull-cap, and slippers, just as they are in pictures and [on stage in] theaters, and just as they were three thousand years ago, no doubt." (56) Twain's report is straight-forward. No noses or slurs, direct or indirect. They are merely part of this exotic, colorful crowd.

"We have had enough of Spain and Gibraltar for the present," crows Twain. "Tangier is the spot we have been longing for all the time." In Tangier, Mark Twain found much to report about its minorities: "There are stalwart Bedouins of the desert here, and stately Moors, proud of a history that goes back to the night of time; and Jews whose fathers fled hither centuries upon centuries ago..." For the Jews Twain reserves the role of refugees. He describes their dress: "Gabardines, sashes about their waists, slippers upon their feet, little skull-caps on the backs of their heads, hair combed down on the forehead, and cut straight from the middle of it from side to side – the self-same fashion their Tangier ancestors have worn for I don't know how many bewildering centuries..." (65–6). Mark Twain seems as fascinated by the long flow of Time of the race represented by these Jews, as by the flow of their gabardines.

That is not to say that Sam Clemens of Hannibal has been entirely cleansed of jibing at Jews. In Tangier, the conventional Shylockian image of Shakespeare's Jew of Venice prancing about his ducats makes a cameo appearance here in the bazaars of Tangier. Mark Twain tells us that the Jewish money-changers "all day long are counting bronze coins from one bushel basket to another," apparently for no other reason than love of handling money, for the coins are 400 or 500 years old and "badly worn and battered" (69–70). Moors and Jews sometimes place themselves under the protection of the Emperor of Morocco, who is a "soulless despot." This gives them the opportunity to "flout their riches in the Emperor's face with impunity" (70–1). Mark Twain reports this with some glee about this moral use of money.

For someone like Mark Twain, who was fascinated by money, there may be a co-existent admiration with a touch of satire in his description of the Jewish money-changer in Tangier:

> On his Sabbath which is Saturday, in contrast to the Mohammedan's on Friday, the Jew shuts up shop; will not touch copper or bronze money at all; soils his fingers with nothing meaner than silver and gold, attends the synagogue devoutly; will not cook or have anything to do with fire; and refrains from embarking on any enterprise. (76)

"Soils his fingers with nothing meaner than silver and gold." Tantalizingly ambiguous. Since his shop is closed, does this refer to the tablewear at his festive meal? Or, is he a hypocritical Jew secretly conducting business, but in deference to the holiness of the day, handles only the more expensive coins? This touch of satire, if that is what Twain intended, implies the money-obsession myth of the Jewish race. But the phrase "at all" can be read as an observation that his general money-changing business policy does not include the baser coins. The rest of the passage seems laudatory: Mark Twain knew about the Jewish Sabbath restrictions and the money-changer fulfills the stringency of the day according to the strict Jewish law.

Twain admires the smoothness of another practice of the Jewish money-changer: The Emperor of Morocco had decreed that only those who can display the vast sum of $100 will be permitted to go on the holy Haj to Mecca. So, "But behold how iniquity can circumvent the law! For a consideration, the Jewish money-changer lends the pilgrim one hundred dollars long enough for him to swear himself through, and then receives it back before the ship sails out of the harbor!" (76). How clever! He gets a fee and the immediate surety of the principal – no waiting, no worry, no problems, no one cheated, except the Moroccan despot. Such iniquity Mark Twain always admired.

In another part of his report, Mark Twain, unwittingly, steps into a possible morass involving noses again: The Jewish "noses are all hooked, and hooked alike. They resemble each other so much that one could almost believe they were of one family." No doubt one can claim that actually emphasizing this feature and its frequency shows Twain's insensitivity about Jews. On the other hand, one can also recognize that the hooked noses and the uniformity of them among the Jews in Tangier is a phenomenon worthy of mention in a journalist's report. It is not gratuitously dragged in, it is certainly not a wicked caricature. It is a fact. It does not seem even to be an ugly feature, for Twain goes on to opine, "Their women are plump and pretty, and do smile upon a Christian in a way which is in the last degree comforting" (66–7), unlike the hostile stares of the Mohammedans. The comforting memory of Adah Menken, perhaps?

This admiration of Jewish women can serve as a transition to the tour's stop in Milan, Italy. While it gave Mark Twain the opportunity to admit that he cannot fathom glib, showy talk about "feeling," "expression," "tone," etc., about Art (192), the unfathomable does pervade this comment of his about the myriad paintings of the Madonna:

> The Italian artists painted Italian Virgins, the Dutch painted Dutch Virgins, the Virgins of the French painters were Frenchwomen – none of them ever put into the face of the Madonna [a Jewess, after all] that indescribable something that proclaims the Jewess, whether you find her in New York, in Constantinople, in Paris, Jerusalem, or in the Empire of Morocco. (194)

In Tangier, Jewish women were merely plump and pretty. It Italy,

Twain endowed them with a racial spirituality. This encomium to Jewish womanhood's specialness should be put in the scale opposite those instances where Twain utters the traditional anti-Jewish slurs that he carried in his unconsciousness and almost unwilled crop up.

In Rome, repelled by the omnipotence of the Church and the omnipresence of churches and priests, Mark Twain imagines what his response would be were he a young native of this old ecclesiastical city. He would travel to America, and upon his return, he would extol America's culture of freedom, equality, and tolerance. Among its democratic wonders of that fabulous country, Twain's imaginary Roman traveler would report, "Common men – men who were neither priests nor princes –...absolutely owned the land they tilled." And, wonder of all wonders, this putative visitor to America would tell his back-home Roman audience:

> Jews, there [in America], are treated just like human beings, instead of dogs. They can work at any business they please, they can sell brand new goods if they want to; they keep drug stores [apparently implying that they are not suspected of maliciously poisoning drugs, as they had been accused of poisoning the wells of Europe]; they can practice medicine among Christians; they can even shake hands with Christians if they choose; they can associate with them, just as one human being does with another human being; they don't have to stay shut up in one corner of the towns; they can live in any part of the town they like best; it is said they even have the privilege of buying land and houses, and owning them themselves, though I doubt that myself [says the amazed modern Roman visitor in his report]; they never have had to run races naked through the public streets, against jackasses, to please the people in carnival time; there they never have been driven by soldiers into a church every Sunday for hundreds of years to hear themselves and their religion especially and particularly cursed; at this very day, in that curious country, a Jew is allowed to vote, hold office, yea, get up on a rostrum in the public street and express his opinion of the government if the government don't suit him! Ah, it is wonderful. (278–9)

Europe had evidently outraged Mark Twain, proud American, and this outrage he expressed through the example of the Jews, the most discriminated-against minority he had met in Europe. They are, perhaps amazingly, the best representation of American freedom that Mark Twain could think of when he wrote this chapter. This panegyric of American democracy, surprisingly does not mention the emancipated Negroes in the Reconstruction period during which *Innocents Abroad* was written, nor the immigrant Irish, who suffered much discrimination in American cities. In this monologue, there is no reference to the unfavorable mythic character of the Jewish race, no criticism, directly or humorously interpolated. The discrimination prejudiciously visited upon them in Europe for centuries has been corrected in the New World's America.

Mark Twain and several companions from among the *Quaker City* tourists decided to forego the voyage from Italy to the port of Jaffa in Palestine. They preferred to approach the Holy Land on the land-route from the north, visiting Istanbul in Turkey and Damascus in Syria and biblical sites on the way. All along, he complained about the heat, the flies, the punishment of their backsides on the haunches of donkeys, the prolixity of tour guides, the Arab security escorts who were more frightening than the bogey-man bandits they were hired to protect the tourists from, relentless "bucksheesh" (tipping) obsequiously demanded, and hordes of pestering mendicants day and night. They quickly became surfeited of ancient ruins, reputedly biblical. To say the least, Twain was negatively impressed with the desolate lands of the Bible, and most deeply repelled by the diseased-ridden populace.

After a fairly miserable journey on the backs of jackasses through Syria, they entered upon the Holy Land. They stopped at Tiberias, on the Sea of Galilee. Writes Twain, "Its people are best examined at a distance. They are particularly uncomely Jews, Arabs, and negroes. Squalor and poverty are the pride of Tiberias" (549). All were victims together of Turkish ineptitude or just plain care-lessness. But the Jews are the subject of a particular observation:

They say that the long-nosed, lanky, dyspeptic-looking body-snatch-
ers [probably another form of vagabonds], with the indescribable
hats on, and a long curl dangling down in front of each ear, are the
old, familiar, self-righteous Pharisees we read of in the Scriptures.
Verily, they look it. Judging merely by their general style, and without other evidence, one might easily suspect that self-rightousness
was their specialty. (550)

Noses again. Long noses, not hooked ones this time. These are again
careful observations of a journalist. However, Mark Twain's preoccupation with the squalor, disease, and noses betrayed him into falling
into the attention of two scholars disturbed by this emphasis.

Sander Gilman, in an article entitled "Mark Twain and the Diseases of the Jews," would have us believe that Twain saw the affliction
of physical blindness among the Jews in the Holy Land as fulfillment
of a Christian doctrine reiterated in the writings of religionists and
pseudoanthropologists of his own time and going back hundreds
of years. As Gilman puts it, the doctrine, as intoned in 2 Peter 1:8–9,
taught that "Those who 'lacketh' knowledge of our Lord Jesus Christ
are 'blind'," and the results are noted in Romans 11.25: "that 'blindness in part is happened to Israel…'"[3] Gilman apparently presumes
Twain came to believe this as a fundamentalist Christian – though,
remarks Allison Ensor in *Mark Twain and the Bible,* as early as 1858,
Mark Twain no longer considered himself a Christian, "quite unorthodox in his religious thought by the time of his departure for Nevada
in 1861."[4] If rejecting Jesus as divine meant blindness, Mark Twain
would have counted himself among those afflicted.

"For Twain," asserts Gilman, "the tracing of disease becomes a
commentary on the role of the Jews in Western civilization [since]
no people is more ancient or remote or diseased than the Jews."[5] But
Gilman offers no text *by Twain* to support his contention. It appears
to be an indictment by accident of proximity-in-time to writings of
contemporary pundits. Notwithstanding the physiognomy of Jewish
noses, Mark Twain described the deplorable condition of the Jews

as precisely the same as those of all the inhabitants of the land: "The population of Jerusalem is composed of Moslems, Jews, Greeks, Latins, Armenians, Syrian, Copts, Abyssinians, Greek Catholics, and a handful of protestants.... Rags, wretchedness, poverty, and dirt, those signs and symbols that indicate the presence of Moslem rule more surely than the crescent flag itself." (612–3) Filth and unsanitary conditions and the policies of the Turks, were the causes of the ecumenical diseases, not religious belief or unbelief.

The closest that Mark Twain comes to connecting the diseases among the population with the history of Christianity is in his description of what happened after Dr. J.B. Birch, of Hannibal, Missouri, as it happened, a member of the tourist group, had ministered to the diseased eyes of a child. Twain recounts that the natives of contemporaneous Palestine "swarmed" to the doctor like the sick of biblical times – "the ancestors of these people precisely like them in color, dress, manners, customs, simplicity" – "flocking" to Jesus in order to be healed (514–5). Gilman would have us understand that, to Mark Twain, "The Arabs of the Holy Land are merely the unchanged biblical Jews in disguise."[6] This clever academic legerdemain suggests the following syllogism based on Gilman's thesis: Mark Twain is under the impression that the Jews' diseases are due to their refusal to accept Jesus as the Messiah; The Arabs suffering diseases in his day are the "unchanged biblical Jews in disguise." Therefore, Mark Twain basically feels that the diseases of the Arabs are due to their refusal to accept Jesus as the Messiah.

I think that this proposition is untenable. Twain simply does not connect disease – among Jews or any people – with religion.

For Andrea Greenbaum, in her article "'A Number-One Troublemaker': Mark Twain's Anti-Semitic Discourse in Concerning the Jews," it is Twain's reference to the long noses of the Jews of Tiberias that springboards her discussion. She assumes that Twain's mention of "long noses" indicates underlying views of a racial nature, and, like Gilman, further assumes that Mark Twain ascribed to the theories of the "pseudoscience of ethnology" (her term) of the late 19th century because they were fashionable in his time. Thus, it seems to her inevitable that he would have been affected by their theories of "The Jew's supposedly defective physiognomy – his hooked nose, dark skin, flat feet,…nasal voice, and neurotic psyche, were illustrative of his racial inferiority" to the Aryan.[7] (By the way, James Russell Lowell, who praised Mark Twain's "Jumping Frog" story as the best humorous piece so far in American literature, thought that Twain's nose "had a long Semitic curve"!)[8] She goes so far as to drag in the anti-Semites' bugaboo of circumcision as a manifestation of the Jews' physical inferiority. This phallic condition is a problem for the pseudoethnologist, not for Mark Twain. He never mentions it. Though Greenbaum seems to feel that Twain had the misfortune to have lived while these savants were publishing their conclusions, she is not able to cite their works in Mark Twain's library or echoes in his writings.[9]

Presumably, Twain differentiated between a long nose and a hooked one, and no nose to speak of, like his description of "Isaac" aboard the *Columbia* in 1867. Some years after this trip to the Holy Land, in 1892, Twain visited Marienbad, a spa like Tiberias for the health-baths, and observed:

> Almost the only striking figure is the Polish Jew. He is very frequent. He is tall and of grave countenance and wears a coat that reaches to his ankle-bones, and he has a little wee curl or two in front of each ear. He has a prosperous look, and seems to be as much respected as anybody.[10]

Here, unlike Twain's description of the Jews in Tangier and Tiberias years before, the racial nose is not mentioned; the dyspeptic countenance has miraculously become "grave"; his dress is still somewhat funny, wearing a long coat to his ankle-bones, but the funny long locks in front of the ears have shrunk to a "little wee curl." Notwithstanding *fin-de-siecle* theories, there seems to be nothing inferior about the Polish Jew. The Polish Jew (as a group, it would seem) "is very frequent." They are "prosperous," with money to spend on a sojourn at the Baths. In both the Holy Land in 1867 and in Austria in 1892, Mark Twain recorded and published what he saw.

Tiberias was not only a haven of Jews with long noses; the city had a Jewish history that fascinated Mark Twain:

> The Sanhedrin [ancient Jewish supreme court of rabbis] met here last, and for three hundred years Tiberias was the metropolis of the Jews in Palestine. It is one of the four holy cities of the Israelites, and it is to them what Mecca is to the Mohammedan and Jerusalem to the Christian. It has been the abiding-place of many learned and famous Jewish rabbins. They lie buried here, and near them lie twenty-five thousand of their faith who traveled far to be near them while they lived and lie with them when they died. The great Rabbi Ben Israel [otherwise unknown] spent three years here in the early part of the third century. He is dead, now. (551)

The gratuitous misplaced touch of intended humor at the end of the passage reeks of the supercilious American interested ultimately in "now-ness." Otherwise, these lines show an almost lyrical wonder, interest, and respect for the city, its history, its Jews, and their "rabbins."

Mark Twain and his companions did see Jerusalem Jews, like their brethren in Tiberias, with long noses, but, unlike in Tangier, few if any, are hooked. We know this from line-drawings of Jerusalem Jews in the time of Twain's visit.[11]

Twain does not mention the noses of Jerusalem's Jews. Indeed, for Mark Twain, Jerusalem was not a Jewish city, but a small, walled locality filled with Christian holy sites and some Mohammedan relics. The Church of the Holy Sepulcher and the Dome of the Rock serve only to whet the Twainian knife of disbelief and sarcasm for slicing through the falsity of the tour guides' palaver. The only authentic Jewish site he mentions is the Western Wall, the wall that retained the hill upon which the Solomonic Temple of the Bible was built:

> At that portion of the ancient wall of Solomon's Temple which is called the Jews' Place of Wailing, and where the Hebrews assemble every Friday to kiss the venerated stones and weep over the fallen

greatness of Zion, any one can see a part of the unquestioned and undisputed Temple of Solomon, the same consisting of three or four stones lying one upon the other, each of which is about twice as long as a seven-octave piano, and about as thick as such a piano is high. (639)

One wonders how many of his readers could have pictured the dimensions of a seven-octave piano. The image is not very apt.

His Hannibal syndrome was only in remission in 1867. The conventional Jewish connection with money again irritated it. A characteristic interpolation occurs in Mark Twain's retelling of the legend of the Wandering Jew in *Innocents Abroad* that he had heard from his tour guide in Jerusalem. According to this version of the tale, he who pushed Jesus away as he stumbled toward the crucifixion and said to him, "Move on," was eternally punished by Jesus who replied, "Move on, thou, also." Since then the Wandering Jew sought death under the swords of Titus's soldiers in the battle of Jerusalem, in the thick of massacres perpetrated by Mohammed in Arabia five hundred years later, and later on during the Crusades, but to no avail. He lived on to become a speculator "in cholera and *railroads*…[and in] infernal machines and patent medicines" (633–5, my italics). How he became a Rothschild-type is not clear.

Every fifty years, this version of the tale goes, the Wandering Jew "must never fail to report in Jerusalem." He wanders through the city, eyeing old landmarks he knew so long ago. Finally he reaches his old house, "and he sheds a few tears at the threshold of his ancient dwelling, and bitter, bitter tears they are. *Then he collects his rent,* and leaves again.… All I have revealed about the Wandering Jew," insists Mark Twain, "can be amply proven by reference to our guide" (635–6, my italics). Of course, no tour guide was likely in 19th-century Jerusalem to present the Wandering Jew as a Rothschild or the ogre in a Jewish-landlord myth. This is Mark Twain-humor of the slip-it-in, deadpan technique he learned from Artemus Ward.

In sum, Jerusalem was, for Mark Twain, a city of squalor and tall tales, stones and buildings that have lost their physical luster and their spirituality, but only for the moment. He concludes his report of his visit:

> The heat will be forgotten, the thirst, the tiresome volubility of the guide, the persecutions of the beggars – and then, all that will be left will be pleasant memories of Jerusalem, memories we shall call up with always increasing interest as the years go by, memories which will some day become all beautiful when the last annoyance that encumbers them shall have faded out of our minds never again to return. (644)

We must remember that when he was revising his travel letters to the *Alta California* for publication in New York in 1869, he had come East to scratch out a place in the sun of the literary world. He actually was in the vanguard of a new literary genre. Mark Twain's "ambitions were not those hallowed in literary Boston," writes Justin Kaplan. "They lay in a still unmapped area bound by journalism, humor, entertainment, and popular literature."[12] In Kenneth Lynn's assessment of what Mark Twain was doing through his Artemus Ward-style of conveying humor in *Innocents Abroad,* lies another important element: This "proud, conscious innocent…[was] prepared to take over the age and judge all nations of the earth by his own."[13]

Since Sam Clemens's days with the Levin boys in Hannibal, the Jews had been an ever-ready target for these nearly automatic quips. The Jews mentioned in his earliest ventures into journalism, his experiences with the individual Jews out west, the Jew on board the ship that brought him to New York did not suggest to him that history transformed this ethnic minority into a sensitive, resilient people. The sojourn in the original habitat of biblical Jews, however, engendered a gleaming of a new sensitivity that marks the ensuing decades. Here is a coherent, vibrant, omnipresent people. In *Innocents Abroad,* he knew what he was doing and to whom he was doing it – but not yet always under his total control. For the next 30 years the balance will tip more and more in favor of the Jews.

Chapter Five
A 30-YEARS' MISCELLANY

D URING THE 30 YEARS after *Innocents Abroad,* from 1870 to the beginning of the 20th century, Mark Twain mentioned Jews in letters, notebooks, sketches, and one major essay, "Concerning the Jews," which requires a chapter for itself. These comments were written not only at home in America but in several European countries to which Twain spent a good deal of time traveling back and forth. (In the next chapter, we shall deal with his relationship with three European Jews.) This span of time includes the "Classical Period" which gives Mark Twain his continued eminence in American and world literature – *Adventures of Tom Sawyer* (1875), The *Prince and the Pauper* (1880) *Life on the Mississippi* (1883), *Adventures of Huckleberry Finn* (1884), *A Connecticut Yankee in King Arthur's Court* (1889). However, of these great works, only one, the autobiographical *Life on the Mississippi,* carries a Jewish persona. The fiction has no character or allusion to anything Jewish, and therefrom hangs a significant anecdote which we shall presently talk about.

1870: On the Bloodthirsty Crusaders
In 1870, Twain served as "Memoranda" editor of the *Galaxy* magazine, a post that gave him free reign to write personal essays, called *feuilletons* in European newspapers and magazines, about any subject

or gripe he may have. One of the latter is his sketch for July, entitled "A Tournament in A.D. 1870." It his reaction to a mock-medieval extravaganza in Lynchburg, Va., which featured dressing-up in medieval costumes and *papier-mache* armor, carefully rehearsed jousts with wooden weapons, and the like. Twain's angry satire on that event pits the mythical "Romance" of chivalry versus the bloody reality of that age by featuring "exhibits" of the paradoxes of conduct during that era that could have been offered at the fair, climaxed by the final paragraph:

> Now, for [our] next exhibition, let us have a fine representation of one of those chivalrous wholesale butcheries and burnings of Jewish woman and children, which the crusading heroes of romance used to indulge in in their European homes, just before starting to the Holy Land, to seize and take to their protection the Sepulchre and defend it from "pollution."[1]

This is not gentle satire. It is a scathing attack upon hypocrisy, hatred, injustice, sham, abuse of might visited upon a persecuted minority. It is the Jews of the 12th century who rose up in Mark Twain's mind to stand as the symbol of guiltless victimization of defenseless people. It also shows, by the way, that Twain gave no thought to the Christ-killing indictment that he had learned about in his Hannibal days, no thought to the punishment due them for their religious intransigence. In the context of this statement, jibes about Jewish obsession for money and any peculiarities of their physiognomy would have paled into merely prejudiced attitudes, and he refrained. In Twain's perspective they are a people that lives apart in the suffering meted out to them so consistently over the centuries.

1870s: On Jewish Acquisitiveness
Nonetheless, one inexplicable thing about Mark Twain's Jews is the inconsistency of his statements. Just a few years after publishing the "memorandum" of atrocities the crusaders perpetrated upon the Jews, Twain returned to the conventional practice of teasing the Jews for

their money-chasing. Louis Harap thinks that Twain (and Charles Dudley Warner) "found a ready symbol in the Jews [in *The Gilded Age* (1873)], who were conspicuous in their numbers and the speed with which they emerged to affluence."[2] This stereotype of the modern Jew will become a favorite that Twain will not be able to overcome entirely. It will serve as a mildly humorous observation, not as a teeth-grinding critique, as in the writings of some of his contemporaries. Indeed, stereotype or not, it may very well be that, unlike these other writers, Mark Twain slyly admired the Jews for it. He baldly stated what we may call his General Philosophy of Acquisitiveness in a sketch entitled "The Revised Catechism" for the New York *Herald Tribune* on September 27, 1871. Twain had written, "What is the chief end of man? to get rich. In what way? – dishonestly if we can; honestly if we must. Who is God, the one only and true? Money is God…." The statement is actually a modern theology, lamentable, un-Christian (which would not have bothered him too much), but true.

Ironically, this cynical universality of belief included Samuel Langhorne Clemens. Quoting Twain's condemnation of modern man's goals, Justin Kaplan asserts, "The code he detested was also, in part, the one he lived by. He wanted to get rich, not just to get along…. It is hard to think of another writer so obsessed in his life and work by the lure, the rustle, and chink and heft of money."[3] Nevertheless, whenever Twain does allude to the Jews' alleged racial lust for lucre, he never sees himself in that mirror.

In this context, is it a favorable or double-edged stereotype Jew of this sort that appears in Mark Twain's notebook for 1879?

> The Jews have the best average brain of any people in the world. The Jews are the only race who work only with their brains and never with their hands. There are no Jew beggars, no Jew tramps, no Jew ditchers, hod-carriers, day-laborers or followers of toilsome, mechanical trade. They are peculiarly and conspicuously the world's intellectual aristocracy.[4]

There's no specific mention here of intellectual contributions to science and medicine, accolades that will come a decade later. At this point, only money talks. Of course, Mark Twain's generalization is woefully incorrect. He should have known better by 1879. He might have – or should have – known that hundreds of Jewish needleworkers in New York City struck the capmakers' shops in 1874 and the cigarmakers' dens in 1877–8, certainly toilsome, mechanical factory jobs. Furthermore, this notebook comment was written by a one-time silver miner who worked physically hard for periods over several years in the Far West to make a fast buck, and was proud of it, though he never made a silver dime from it. It is hard to tell whether he's applauding the Jews or criticizing their anti-hard labor predilection or simply reporting the impressions he had from hearsay sources. Philip Foner, discussing Mark Twain as a social critic, reports that this entry in his notebook was never published in his lifetime – fortunately, Foner adds, because "with a twist or a turn, such praise could be used to support the false charges of anti-Semitic propagandists that the Jews shrewdly live off other's labors."[5]

1883/4: The "Israelite" in *Life on the Mississippi* / the "Uncles" in *Huckleberry Finn*

The truth is, however, that such a Jew does appear in *Life on the Mississippi* (1883). Tangentially discussing the post-Civil War "grouty" relationship between the planter and former negro slaves, Twain observes that the planter, the owner of the farm, will not keep a store to supply the negro's needs, "but let's that privilege to some thrifty Israelite, who encourages the thoughtless negro and wife to…buy on credit" items that are, to begin with, unnecessary and costly. The result is, Twain concludes, that the negro is discouraged and dissatisfied and only "fatten[s] the Israelite for a season," who will then simply move on to another locality and play the game again.[6] There is no further comment by Twain about this cruel practice. The generic, nose-curling term "Israelite" says it all. It is a carry-over from the letters to the *Alta California* from the San-Francisco to New York voyages, an appellation he considered suitable for the obnoxious character he had met on board at that time

It is not an *ad hominem* identification of a specific renegade Jew here either, but clearly a generalization of the race. Yet when opportunity was very much alive to carry over these traits to fictional characters, Mark Twain refrained from doing so.

Under his pen at the time that he was writing about the "Israelite" in *Life on the Mississippi* were the adventures of Huckleberry Finn. A good portion of this classic is devoted to the adventures of two rapacious rapscallions, the Duke and the Dauphin, scam artists living off the innocence of the ignorant. These two characters were no less loving of lucre than the "Israelite." They were equally heartless, playing the ignorant of small towns along the river as the "Israelite" played the poor, ignorant Negro. The rascals set into motion a heartless plan to rip off just-orphaned, unsophisticated, inexperienced, trusting young girls of their inheritance by becoming their "uncles" from overseas. What an opportunity to emulate Dickens's creation of Fagin the Jew, the figure of overweening cupidity, in the ever-popular *Oliver Twist*! Or to ape what successful activist Christian novelists in America were currently doing all around Twain, fattening their own bank accounts by creating avaricious Jewish persona to destroy or convert.

How is it that the everlasting success of Dickens or the immediate popularity of the scribblers did not suggest converting the Duke and the Dauphin in *Huckleberry Finn* into Jews? Perhaps the answer to that question can be found in the following anecdote.

1885: Suzy Clemens's "Biography"

That in Mark Twain's published fiction in the years surrounding the appearance of *Life on the Mississippi* no Jewish character, allusion, or remark appears did not go unnoticed by his readership. The widespread anti-Jewish fiction being read at the time makes the absence a ray of light in the literary darkness. In her proposed "biography" of her famous father, Mark Twain's 13-year-old daughter, Suzy, reports that one day, *circa* 1885, a friend of the family,[7] asked Mark Twain how it is that he "was the only great humorist who had ever written without poking some fun against a Jew."

[Writes young Suzy] Papa at first did not know why it was that he had never spoken unkindly of the Jews in any of his books, but after thinking awhile he decided that the Jews had always seemed to him a race much to be respected; also they had suffered much, and had been greatly persecuted, so to ridicule or make fun of them seemed to be like attacking a man that was already down. And of course that fact took away whatever there was funny in the ridicule of a Jew.[8]

One is reminded that after graphically inflicting satiric stabs into "Isaac," the despised Israelite on board the *San Francisco*, Mark Twain made a similar humanitarian comment at that Jew's downfall. Regardless of intermittent indications otherwise, the silence of the missed opportunity in his creative years speaks of his basic humanity. It must be taken as evidence that an anti-Semitic tendency, either conventional or religious, purposeful or thoughtless, was never an aberration in Twain's creative mind. He was no Charles Dickens. The nefarious uncles in *Huckleberry Finn* remained, quite clearly, gentiles.

1884 Consistency and its Fallacies

Originally, the essay entitled "Consistency" was a *post-mortem* speech delivered in Hartford, Conn., following the election of Grover Cleveland in 1884.[9] Upon reading it, one might be reminded of another American writer who wrote on "consistency" under the title of "Self-Reliance," Ralph Waldo Emerson. Emerson was not Mark Twain's favorite author, to say the least, although Twain knew of his standing in American culture. His one encounter with the New England sage, at the famous dinner in 1877 in honor of Whittier, was a disaster Twain never stopped cringing under. The only reason Emerson's essay might be recalled here is that one sentence in it can be read as a gloss on Mark Twain's essay. Wrote the Concord Sage, "A foolish consistency is the hobgoblin of little minds, adored by little statesmen and philosophers and divines."[10] With equal elan, all three types were flayed by Mark Twain in "Consistency."

Twain, like Emerson, does not define or exemplify what is a *fool-*

ish consistency. It is enough for him to ask, "So long as he is loyal to his best self, what should he care for other loyalties?"[11] Twain comes to the general conclusion:

> I am persuaded that the world has been tricked into adopting some false and most pernicious notions about consistency – and to such a degree that the average man has tuned the rights and wrongs of things entirely around, and is proud to be "consistent," unchanging immovable, fossilized, where it should be his humiliation that he is so."[12]

It is a rather amazing coincidence that Twain metaphorized consistency as a fossil and Arnold Toynbee, the eminent historian, many years later once metaphorized the consistency of the Jewish people with the same paleontological condition as a "fossil" of an ancient civilization. And this is what Mark Twain had to say about the Jews in this essay on "Consistency":

> When a man who has been brought up as a Jew becomes a Christian, the Jews sorrow over it and reproach him for his inconstancy; all his life he has denied the divinity of Christ, but now he makes a lie of his past; upon him rests the stigma of inconsistency; we can never be sure of him again. We put in the deadly parallel columns what he said formerly and what he says now, and his credit is gone. We say, Trust him not; we know him now; he will change again; and possibly again and yet again; he has no stability.[13]

On first reading, this can be taken as a high compliment to the Jews, but the context in which the statement appears transforms it into a harsh critique. "Loyalty to petrified opinions [Mark Twain asserts] never yet broke a chain or freed a human soul in this world – and never will."[14] The Jewish example is Twain's most extended one among Presbyterian, Buddhist, Baptist, Democrat, and Republican petrified groups.

However, the essay is a curious fulcrum between past and future pronouncements by Mark Twain on the subject of consistency. We might remember that years before, Twain berated Bret Harte for not acknowledging his Jewish birth; indeed, it was Harte's worst crime in Twain's estimation. And in the future, in an essay Twain will write in Vienna in 1897, "Stirring Times in Austria", he will exemplify that non-conformity to Jewish peoplehood in the form of assimilation did not prevent Jews from being "roasted" in all continental nations, by all groups in them. He martyrized them. In "Concerning the Jews," the companion essay (1898), he will imply, with admiration, that it was racial consistency that prevented ancient empires, all now defunct, from annihilating the Jewish race.

Did Mark Twain simply forget in Vienna what he had said in that earlier address in Hartford, Conn.? Or change his mind about its thesis? Non-conformity might have sounded attractive in 1884, but misdirected for Jewish realities of 1897–8 in Europe. Fortunately, he may have intuited immediately that the application of his doctrine of non-conformity to the unique place of Jews in the western world was misplaced. This may very well be the reason he never published "Consistency." It was left to literary executors to do so.

1886–9: On "Shylocks" and "Pirates"

The losing venture of *Ah Sin* with Bret Harte did not cure Mark Twain from trying to transform his fiction into drama. He became involved with Daniel Frohman, of Sandusky, Ohio, a midwesterner like himself, who became the foremost theatrical producer on Broadway, operating out of the Lyceum Theatre. In 1886, Frohman produced a stage-version of *Colonel Sellers* culled from Twain's *The Gilded Age*. As usual, Twain, who did not trust publishers of his books, was equally leery of producers of his plays. In a letter of May 13, 1886, he complains about "go[ing] through the profound wisdom of tying myself to an actor with a gold thread, & tying the actor to a Hebrew manager [Daniel Frohman]."[15]

In time he sued Frohman. He called the producer "that Lyceum Theater Jew,"[16] which sounds pretty anti-Jewish, in a letter to H.H. Rogers, his personal financial adviser. However, Frohman recalls in his memoirs that "Mr. Clemens and I played our nightly games of pool at the Players with unruffled amity" during the litigation,[17] which takes away the sting of any real anti-Jewish animosity in the unfortunate remark. It is again an instance of the Hannibal syndrome, like the Old Faithful geyser, automatically gushing out.

Mark Twain was deep in a financial hole about this time. He owed money to a non-Jewish creditor, and now complained that the creditor wanted every penny paid back, plus interest. In a letter to Rogers (March 15, 1898), he draws a convoluted analogy: "I didn't know [Barrow, the creditor] was holding out for *interest*. If I had known that, it would have hardened this Pharaoh [meaning himself] again[st] that child of Israel [the creditor]."[18] And why did Twain call Barrow a "child of Israel"? The answer may be found in a sequel letter (May 31, 1898), "So far as I know, he is the only similarly-situated creditor in all history since Shylock's time who has demanded blood in addition to flesh."[19]

Though Twain's memory of *The Merchant of Venice* is a bit faulty, it is no surprise that Shakespeare's character sprang automatically into his mind. Shylock was a wide-spread stereotype for the lucre-loving Jewish persona in 19th century American anti-Semitism. Shakespeare's humanization of the character was conveniently forgotten. "It was not the human aspect of Shylock," Louis Harap noted, "it was his preoccupation with money and his inhuman hatred of the Christian."[20] There were what Jonathan Sarna calls "conversionists" who were "motivated to take Jews out of their upper status as 'Shylocks,'" thereby solving the Jewish problem.[21] The sectarian-tainted background of the popular fear and dislike of this Jewish prototype did not count at all in Twain's mind. Even regarding Shylock's preoccupation with money, we ought by now to recognize Twain's schizophrenic view of Jewish money-loving as both abhorrent and admirable, symbolized here in the conventional figure of Shylock.

It reflects David Gerber's insight that the "Jewish capitalist" in 19th-century American anti-Semitism was sometime embodied in "the public consciousness as Shylock," whereas "The Gentile capitalist may be regarded as a cultural hero."[22] Such a hero to Mark Twain was H.H. Rogers, the financier whose advice and help saved Twain from embarrassment or worse after his financial ruin: "He's a pirate all right," said Mark Twain, "but he owns up to it and enjoys being a pirate. That's the reason I like him."[23] The spectral Shylock never stopped haunting Mark Twain, and Shylock will yet again appear in his work as a stereotype. But powerful and everlasting though Shylock be as an evocation of cupidity, Twain will never give him the admired status of a real financial pirate.

Chapter Six

A TRIAD OF EUROPEAN JEWS

FROM 1894 to the birth of the new century, Mark Twain commuted back and forth from America to Europe – that is, England, France, Germany, Austria-Hungary. In these countries, he was lionized as the Great American Humorist, and, as Carl Dolmetsch's book on Mark Twain in Vienna and Kenneth Lynn's survey of his humor indicate, he was not entirely satisfied that his serious writings were hardly noticed and the serious intent of his humor rarely understood; nonetheless, he was entirely ready to welcome and thoroughly enjoy the acclamation anyway. In continental Europe, he also encountered three prominent Jews – each becoming prominent for entirely discrete reasons: prominence was thrust upon Alfred Dreyfus by a spurious indictment of espionage because he was a Jew; Theodor Herzl thrust himself into fame as the political savior of the Jewish nation; and Sigmund Freud immortalized himself by discovering a world within the mind.

It was their fate and Mark Twain's to become entwined, by ways that none had preplanned.

1894 (to 1899): Mark Twain and the Dreyfus Affair

On October 15, 1894, the French Army catapulted France into a turmoil that lasted ten years. It arrested Capt. Alfred Dreyfus for treason on behalf of Germany. He was convicted and sentenced to life on Devil's Island, an infamous penal colony off French Guiana. Everyone knew that one of the major factors in the arrest was that Dreyfus was Jewish, since it was also widely suspected that he was framed. The country split down the middle, one side claiming justice must be done, the other side countering that the Army must be in the right, because an attack upon the Army is an attack on *La France* itself. Mark Twain, who happened to be in France in 1894, was swept into the agitation. By 1897, he was deeply involved. In November, he was planning a book about Dreyfus; by February 1898, the first chapter was actually written, but the project was never completed. French governments fell because of the continuous and vociferous agitation in the press, on the streets, among politicians, and even among families. On January 13, 1898, Emile Zola brought the cauldron to a boil with the pro-Dreyfusard, front-page open letter in the *Aurora,* Clemenceau's newspaper (which gave it much more authority), entitled *J'Accuse.* The uproar in the French parliament forced the government to place one of its primary authors on trial, and to convict him of libel. Zola was supported by Anatole France and Marcel Proust, among many intellectuals. One of those intellectuals was Mark Twain, who hated the French anyway. He cabled the *New York Herald Tribune,* January 14, 1898: "Such cowards, hypocrites, and flatterers as the members of [French] military and ecclesastical courts the world could produce by the million every year. But it takes five centuries to produce a Joan of Arc or a Zola."[1]

Twain never met Alfred Dreyfus. From a letter written September 15, 1899 to American-Jewish historian Simon Wolf, it is clear that he knew all along that Dreyfus was a Jew, and agreed with the strategy not to center pro-Dreyfus agitation on that point: "Jews did wisely [he wrote] in keeping quiet during the Dreyfus agitation – the other course would have hurt Dreyfus's cause, and I see now that *nothing* could have helped it."[2] Given Twain's avowed feeling that the Jews had had a belly-full of persecution over the centuries, that Dreyfus was a Jew may have been an additional private incentive to take up literary cudgels in his defense. But widespread anti-Jewish feeling among the

French made it unstrategic to proclaim this underlying cause of the indictment publicly.

In sketches and letters to newspapers back in the U.S., Twain never failed to excoriate "French justice." Whether it was appropriate or not to the topic under his pen, he dragged in the Dreyfus Affair. Four very variegated examples: In a humorous sketch published in 1899, entitled "My First Lie, and How I Got Out of It," Twain complains, "From the beginning of the Dreyfus case to the end of it, all France, except a couple of dozen moral paladins, lay under the smother of the silent assertion – lie that no wrong was being done to a persecuted and un-offending man."[3] ("Persecuted" served as the "buzz-word" to point to the fact that the legal-shrouded indictment of Dreyfus hid the anti-Semitic sentiment of the French General Staff). In another essay in which he meditated on the loss of "My Boyhood Dreams," Twain asks rhetorically, "Who can understand why a person should have an ambition to belong to the French army," and after discoursing further on the phenomenon of boyhood dreaming, interjects, "Perhaps we can put ourselves in his place and respect his dream – Dreyfus's [I mean]."[4] After the second trial (1899) in which it was proved that his original accusers perjured themselves by using forged documents, Dreyfus was incredibly declared guilty again – as a sop, his sentence was drastically reduced. Twain wrote a devastating satirical fantasy set in a futuristic America ("From the 'London Times' of 1904") on the logic of French justice. The piece is somewhat belabored, but its purpose is clear. Twain imagines a case before the Supreme Court in which the Court decides that a living person is indeed dead, as a satire on the cruel absurdity of the French court's decision.[5] In another satirical sketch – this one hilarious – "American Representation in Austria" (1899), Twain intends to haul the new American Minister over satiric coals as inept and ignorant. During a purported conversation with him, Twain finds it heavy going to unearth a subject upon which the new diplomat can talk.

> "...You tug out another remark, this time on the all-absorbing topic, the stirring topic, the topic which is inflaming two worlds – the Dreyfus case.

> There is a halting, disjointed, uninterested, ignorant reply, and you realize that the Envoy Extraordinary and Minister Plenipotentiary of the United States of America knows nothing about the matter.[6]

This, to Mark Twain, is evidently nearly criminal.

That Dreyfus was indeed Jewish and this fact did not dissuade Mark Twain from fighting his battle for years says something about the difference in his mind about humorous interpolations of an anti-Jewish nature and his serious view of the Jewish question. The sentiments that Suzy reported her father harbored seem borne out by his continual participation in the Dreyfus Affair. As a journalist, it would be expected that he would write about the Affair now and again, but his persistence, his actual creating opportunities to do so in published articles, speak against any allegation that anti-Semitism was hidden in a niche in his mind. Who knows to what extent Mark Twain's holding *La France's* face up to the mirror of demeaning laughter influenced the French to restore Dreyfus to his Army rank, privileges, and pension in 1906. That Dreyfus accepted his rank and served as best he could thereafter, says more about the loyalty of this Jew to France, than the loyalty of France to its Jews.

That another journalist became convinced of that would have worldwide repercussions.

1894: Mark Twain and Theodor Herzl

It is a piquant coincidence that in 1894 Mark Twain came into contact with no less a Jewish personality than Theodor Herzl, who was to be so deeply influenced by the Dreyfus Affair. They met in Paris – the rough product of the American West, whose previous involvement with individual Jews was two Western characters, and a theatrical producer out of a small Midwestern city, and the elegant, almost dandy, polished product of cosmopolitan, sophisticated Vienna, capital of the Austrian-Hungarian Empire. Mark Twain was already famous in Europe as journalist, humorist, and novelist; Theodor Herzl was climbing the ladder of fame as the writer of *feuilletons* and, since 1891,

Paris correspondent for his newspaper, the Vienna *Neue Freie Presse*. There was a common ground between them – the Dreyfus case – but there is no indication that they discussed it. And it was too early in the arousal of Herzl's Zionism for them to discuss that topic, but Twain will react to it in time.

The occasion of their coming together was reported in a humorous *feuilleton* that Herzl wrote in German, of course, for his newspaper.[7] It was announced that the famous Mark Twain was going to read from his works at a British embassy "recital" in Paris, and Herzl (*perhaps* at the request of a fellow journalist, as he humorously claims in his *feuilleton*) went to review it.

Up to now in this study, we have analyzed what Mark Twain had said about the Jewish race and individual Jews with whom he became acquainted. Now we shall have the opportunity of seeing what a Jew says about Mark Twain. In his *feuilleton,* Herzl relates that on the way to the embassy he got on a bus that was filled with chattering British school girls on an outing to hear the fabled writer from the fabled land – the American West. Few men were present in the hall, and Herzl was not above penning some words of admiration for the young and older ladies who dominated the audience. Finally, Mark Twain appears:

> A smallish, slim, somewhat slovenly looking man [Herzl wrote], with artistic grey locks, a thick mustache hanging under a hooked nose [Mark Twain seems not to have been able to avoid hooked noses, including his own!], a blank gaze, flabby cheeks, and a pointed chin....bushy protruding eyebrows that twirl upwards and which indicate at once both the good and the stinging nature in Mark Twain.

Herzl found Twain's humor to be "something immense, overpowering, and shattering," worthy of the "respect and veneration" he receives. "He is indeed a remarkable reader," but not for the subjects he chose, nor for his own works: "Samuel Clemens does not know how to recite Mark Twain's sketches." By acting as a comedian, Twain makes his sketches something different from what they are intended to be. And Herzl, in a humorous Appendix to his sketch, says he told as much to "Clemens, old boy." That is hard to believe. The end of the *feuilleton* has him shake Mark Twain's hand as they part. This, maybe. After all, both were practicing journalists.

The familiarity with which Herzl wrote his *feuilleton* comes from a familiarity with Mark Twain's works. Back in 1882, Herzl penned a note in his diary wherein he discusses a collection of Twain's stories and remarks that the translation is inadequate for Twain's humor and bite. Two years after the recital in Paris, Herzl alludes to Mark Twain in an unlikely setting. By 1896, Herzl had already undertaken his Zionist leadership as a reaction to the Dreyfus trial, and he had an audience with the Grand Duke of Baden, a noble close to the German Kaiser. The two discussed Herzl's plan of a Jewish homeland in Palestine and got down to the nitty-gritty of financial support (the duke was afraid of the exodus of money if a great number of Jews went on *aliyah*). On this, Herzl records in his diary:

> To illustrate the psychology of the worker: I told him Mark Twain's story about Tom Sawyer: how one Sunday afternoon [Herzl's memory betrayed him; it was a Saturday] Tom was condemned as a punishment to paint his father's [incorrect; it was Aunt Polly's] fence, and how he got out of it. He did not say to his comrades "I *must*," but "I am *allowed* to paint the fence." Then they all insisted on being allowed to help him. No doubt the Duke appreciated the story.[8]

Herzl and Mark Twain were to meet again when the Twain family came to Vienna in 1897. Twain immediately adhered to the circle of Viennese journalists and intelligensia, mostly Jewish, including Theodor Herzl. They went to German-language plays together and played a card-game called "tarok" together. Twain's relationship with Herzl became fairly close.[9] On October 31, 1897, at the prestigious Concordia Hall, Mark Twain gave a speech to an audience of the Vienna elite, including Herzl – no review of this event by Herzl is known.[10] More significantly, Twain was at a performance of Herzl's drama, *Das Neue Ghetto, The New Ghetto,* on January 5, 1898. Roiling in Twain's mind were the Dreyfus Affair, the raucous anti-Semitism he had heard in a session of the Austrian Parliament (see next chapter), the horrendous anti-Jewish riots in Prague. The plot of Herzl's play concerns an assimilated Jew (that is, one freed from the restraints of the ancient, inherited ghetto) who is snubbed by a Christian friend with political ambitions because it is not politic to be connected to a Jew. The Jew dies in a duel with a Jew-baiter, but is reconciled on his deathbed with his penitent friend. Guilt-ridden, this friend realizes that the walls of "the new ghetto" must be universally breached. So impressed was Mark Twain with this intensely Jewish-problem play that a few months later he began to translate it into English, and even urged his financial adviser in New York, H.H. Rogers, to gather money for its production. Rogers refused, giving America's war with Spain as an excuse for the lack of money. The project lapsed.[11]

It must be remarked that Mark Twain's previous flirtations with theatrical projects involved his own writings – transforming passages of his published material into plays, and was invariably humorous. Here we have him interested in a vehicle that is not American, nor originally in English, nor his own, nor humorous. And its hero is an unoffending Jew and the potential villain is a Christian ready to compromise his friendship with the Jew for personal, political gain. This is a complete reversal of all popular conceptions of the Jew as the prime symbol of aggressive venality. Yet Mark Twain considered it as a project upon which he was willing to work, if only circumstances in New York would make it feasible. This does not comport with accusations that he was in any way anti-Semitic. Nor can it be argued that Twain's primary interest in Herzl's play was the motif of intolerance of the defenseless. There was always the freed Negro who would have made a well-known if uncommon subject for a play on such a theme, but somehow it never attracted Mark Twain.

Herzl's Zionism and Mark Twain's interest in the Jewish race connected also in 1898, but that discussion we will defer at this time. Sufficient for the moment to say that Twain was ambivalent about the Zionist enterprise, but did admire the boldness, initiative, and self-confidence of his Viennese friend. These are qualities that Mark Twain admired ever since he was Sam Clemens.

1897 ff.: Sigmund Freud and Mark Twain

The reversal of personalities in this subtitle indicates the flow of relationship. Mark Twain never mentions Sigmund Freud, but Freud does mention Mark Twain in several of his writings.

Carl Dolmetsch in his book *"Our Famous Guest": Mark Twain in Vienna* records the occasions when these two men came together at card game sessions, special occasions (see his index), and theater (especially the night both saw *The New Ghetto*).[12] It is also possible that the Clemenses visited Dr. Freud in his capacity as a famous Viennese neurologist, on behalf of daughter Jean, who showed signs of epilepsy, but this has not been verified in their records.[13]

Freud actually used tales and sketches by Mark Twain in his scholarly essays to exemplify points of his theories. For example, to exemplify "the economy of pity" Freud offered humorous portions of *Roughing It*, "A Burlesque Biography," and a passage from *Innocents Abroad* (chapter 27: "Rare Sport. Guying the Guides"), from which Freud concludes that the "small contribution of humor that we produce ourselves are as a rule made at the cost of anger – instead of getting angry."[14] Perhaps Freud has unwittingly given us a defense of Mark Twain's Hannibal syndrome. That Mark Twain contributed to the new science of psychoanalysis is a fact that would have astonished and amused him.

Freud's regard for Mark Twain during the latter's stay in Vienna is emphasized in a letter Freud wrote on February 9, 1898. Dr. Freud played "truant" from a lecture by the chief physician to Prince Bismarck – a politically important event – and added, "I treated myself to listening to our old friend Mark Twain in person, which was a sheer delight." Twain's lecture was entitled, "How to Steal a Watermelon," not a title to attract the intelligensia. We can appreciate Freud's audacity in making his choice when we read Mark Twain's smug remark in his own letter about the event, "Six members of the Imperial family [were] present and four princes of lesser degree, and I taught the whole of them how to steal watermelons."[15]

The sad climax of their relationship occurred twenty-eight years after Mark Twain died. The year is 1938; the locale is London, England. Sigmund Freud, an exile from *anschlussed* Vienna, ill with cancer, is living out the last months of his life He was asked to contribute to a collection of essays on anti-Semitism. He did. A good deal of his essay, however, was comprised of quotations from an uncited source. He admitted, "I can no longer recall where I read the essay of which I made a précis nor who was its author."[16] The mystery was solved in 1980 by Marion A. Richmond, in "The Lost Source in Freud's Comment on Anti-Semitism: Mark Twain." After nearly 40 years, Freud had dredged up from his memory Mark Twain's "Concerning the Jews," published in 1899. Evidently, Freud did not detect any vapor of anti-Jewishness in that essay.

Neither Herzl nor Freud were at all bothered by the anti-Jewish slights that Mark Twain had slipped into *Innocents Abroad* and *Life on the Mississippi*, both of which were well-known in German editions.[17] On the contrary, they both – one, an aggressive observer of anti-Semitism in Europe, the other an analyst of the phenomenon – admired his humor without reservations, and actually cited passages from his writings in their own. His relationship with both of them is perhaps the most stringent test thus far of Twain's mastery of the lessons of Artemus Ward, to surprise but not to offend. And also whether, in the eyes of these meta-sensitive Jewish intellectuals, he was anti-Jewish. Evidently, he passed both tests.

Chapter Seven

SHOCK TREATMENT IN VIENNA

T HE CLEMENS FAMILY arrived in Vienna on September 27, 1897, for a two-year stay. From Carl Dolmetsch's description of the event in his magnificently researched book, *"Our Famous Guest": Mark Twain in Vienna,* one would think that a grand potentate from some mysterious enclave on the Persian Gulf had come to grace the city. The press heralded his coming and the intelligentsia entered into a state of expectant anticipation. Once settled, it took Mark Twain but a short time to be absorbed into the mainly Jewish conglomerate of intellectuals. Dolmetsch notes that "a foreign writer [would] find his collegial acquaintanceship in *fin de siecle* Vienna to be preponderantly Jewish, given the disproportionate representation of Jews in the arts and journalism in the city." The star-studded cast included his friend Theodor Herzl in journalism and in drama, along with Schnitzler and Siegmund Schlesinger in theater, Mahler and Schönberg in music, and Sigmund Freud, in medicine.[1] Twain had begun learning German in America for a trip to Germany in the late 1870s and improved it on subsequent trips. By 1897, Twain knew German quite well and so could navigate easily in their midst.[2]

He was avidly sought after for interviews, and most of the interviewers he deigned to sit with were Jewish, or were employed by Jewish-owned newspapers. "Those seemingly excluded," Dolmetsch notes, "were published by gentiles, and, in some cases…overtly anti-Semitic."[3] It is not to be wondered that this was the situation. Mark Twain's daughter, Clara, recalls in her biography of her father published in 1931: "Father had always been a great admirer of the Jewish race and now had the opportunity in Vienna to test and prove the soundness of his good opinion of that great people."[4]

A month into his stay in the Austrian capital and immediate exposure to individual Jews – attracted to them perhaps because they were not only modernized, but assimilationist – seemed to confirm what Clara said was "always" his opinion about the Jewish race. Already in a letter dated October 23, 1897, to Reverend Joseph Twitchell, a Hartford clergyman and a special friend, Twain expatiates:

> It is Christian and Jew by the horns [here in Mittel Europa] – the advantage with the superior man, as usual – the superior man being the Jew every time and in all countries. Land, Joe, what chance would the Christian have in a country where there were three Jews to ten Christians…The difference between the brain of the average Christian and that of the average Jew – *certainly in Europe* – is about the difference between the tadpole's and an Archbishop's. It's a marvelous race – by long odds the most marvelous that the world has produced, I suppose.[5]

Mark Twain had no compunction (or pity) about expressing these observations to a Christian minister. One wonders what the Reverend Mr. Twitchells's thoughts were as he faced his congregation the Sunday after receiving this missile.

It did not take Mark Twain long to become a star in the Viennese galaxy. On the 31st of October, he was the chief speaker to address the Concordia Club, an elite literary organization that boasted most of the vaunted intellectuals of the city. Dolmetsch reports it had 348 members at the time, of whom 150 were Jewish (which inspired anti-Semitic journalists to form their own club).[6] Facing these high-powered Jewish Germanophiles, Twain felt comfortable enough (again relying on what he learned from Artemus Ward) to deliver a talk in German on

"The Difficulties of the German Language" (or, as some translated the title, "The Horrors of the German Language.") The audience, scintillating with luminaries, laughed heartily with him, and Twain's talk was a great success.[7] His next plunge, however, was into Viennese reality.

The Reichsrat and the Jews

Perhaps a mutual connection with Bret Harte inspired Bettina Wirth, a writer of novels and a translator of Harte, to arrange a ticket for Twain to attend the October 28, 1897, session of the Reichsrat, the Austrian Parliament.[8] It was an educational experience for Mark Twain, journalist. It flung him into a cauldron of European realities that never confronted him in the halcyon adventure he described in the first volume of *Innocents Abroad,* thirty years earlier. Furthermore, it was a material-gathering event for a piece he could send back to a magazine in America. The result was "Stirring Times in Austria", published in *Harper's,* March 1898.

The Hapsburg Empire at the time was made up of nineteen or twenty nations, each with its own concerns, aspirations, and intrigues. It was vastly anomalous – for example, the Emperor of Austria and the Empire was simultaneously the King of Hungary, one of the constituent nations. But it generally worked: The relative tranquillity enjoyed by the Empire was the result of trade-offs between the government in Vienna and each regional, quasi-autonomous government. As Twain observed, they all hated the government in Vienna, but hated each other more. Their representatives in the Reichsrat numbered 425, from all the Empire's walks of life – princes, counts, lawyers, priests, peasants, etc. "They are religious men; they are earnest, sincere, devoted, and they hate the Jews."[9] Among all the checks and balances that glued the legislators together, this was a special bond.

The sitting that Mark Twain attended was an all-night session in the throes of considering a language bill: to permit Bohemia (today's Czech Republic) to replace German with Czech as the official language of the country, a trade-off accepted by the government. This inflamed the volatile opposition of die-hard Germanophiles and the session was predicted to be a particularly exciting one. It was.

One of its memorable features was a 12-hour address by a Dr. Lecher against the measure. Another was what Mark Twain called "curious parliamentary etiquette."[10] For a collaborator of *The Gilded Age,* which contains passages of curious practices of American Congressmen, those of the Austrian Reichsrat had to be curious indeed to impress him. They were, and Mark Twain reports them at length.

The general disorder and palpable disrespect for the President of the Parliament and for the speaker on the floor and for one another were obvious, ear-shattering, and total. Side arguments pervaded the air (but did not prevail upon the speaker who had the floor – he simply droned on). For an education on the topic of Austrian legislators' maledictions upon their colleagues, it is worth reading Twain's essay.

The bedlam featured cliche epithets and name-calling and second-class insults. First-class insults featured epithets about the Jews, and Mark Twain reports them faithfully. For example, the worst that Member of Reichsrat Wholmeyer can think of to respond to an insult by his colleague Wolf, a particularly galling opponent, is, "You Jew, you!" Representative Vielohlawek takes this as a cue to fling at Wolf, "I would rather take my hat off to a Jew than to Wolf!" He is joined by Strobach, who yells at Wolf, "Jew flunky! Here we have been fighting the Jews for ten years and now you are helping them to power again! How much do you get for it?" (Alongside the vague insight into anti-Jewish Austrian history is obviously heard the old slur about the Jew's venality). A greatly appreciated taunt by one legistator to another, translated from the German as, "Your grandmother was conceived on a dunghill" was overwhelmed by a booming chant: *"Schmul lieb' Kohn! Schmul lieb' Kohn! Schmul lieb' Kohn"* The one civilized taunt was Klotzenbauer's: "'Holofernes, where is Judith?' [Storm of laughter]" (Twain's brackets),[11] which demonstrates, at least, that some Austrian lawmakers knew something of the Jewish Apocrypha.

Ultimately, fights broke out on the floor and troops were called in to restore order. "It was an odious spectacle – odious and awful" laments Mark Twain, thorough democrat, witnessing the dragging of "representatives of a nation" forcibly out of the hall of legislation, out of the building, into the street. The political consequences were grave: the government fell and riots broke out in Vienna and "there were three or four days of furious rioting in Prague…. The Jews and Germans were harried and plundered and their houses destroyed," relates Twain, "…in some cases the Germans being the rioters, in others the Czechs – and in all cases the Jew had to roast, no matter which side he was on."[12] As far as Mark Twain was concerned, apparently, things haven't changed much for the Jews in Mittel Europa in 700 years. In his 1870 newspaper sketch on a staged modern medieval extravaganza, it will be remembered, he stressed that they were the particular innocent targets of the Crusaders' extra-curricular activities in the 12th century.

Incidentally, this was the "December storm" of 1897 that Ernest Pawel describes in his biography of Franz Kafka. Kafka as a "hypersensitive and guiltridden" boy of *bar mitzva* age witnessed it, and, opines Pawel, "it seems inconceivable for the incident not to have left its mark" on him. Cynthia Ozick makes the connection, indirect as it may be, by quoting Twain's statement about the Prague riots in her essay "The Impossibility of Being Kafka."[13] It was to have left its mark on Mark Twain, too, for "Stirring Times in Austria" was destined to be the stimulus for an unplanned sequel in which Twain was to make his major statement about the Jewish race.

Chapter Eight

CONCERNING "CONCERNING THE JEWS"

THE GESTATION OF THIS ESSAY, "Concerning the Jews," written 1898, published 1899, may have taken nearly a decade. Back in 1890, Mark Twain had been invited by the editor of the *American Hebrew*, a New York weekly, to contribute to a symposium of Christian clergy and intellectuals on "reasons and remedies for anti-semitism." The respondents were asked to consider four aspects: (1) personal experience of any justification for prejudice towards individual Jews; (2) the role of religious instruction in church and Sunday school that the Jewish race is "despised" because of their rejection and crucifying of Jesus; (3) the conduct of business by the Jew vis-a-vis that of his Christian competitor; (4) suggestions to cure "the existing prejudice."[1]

One wonders what drove the editor to invite Mark Twain to join such a symposium. There was nothing published by Twain as yet to suggest his interest in the subject. Undoubtedly, it was the fact that such a statement from him would represent a man and writer who in his own day achieved the status as the typical, almost mythic, American – born in the mid-west, alumnus of the far-west, champion of racial tolerance, and wise-man/humorist of life's experiences.

Carl Dolmetsch acknowledges that a statement by Twain had been written but he doesn't know why the piece was never published by the *American Hebrew,* and lets it go at that.[2] Now we conjecture: He wrote it, laid it aside, and John S. Tuckey found it. In 1972, he published it as Appendix A to his collection, *Mark Twain's "Fables of Man."* This statement is in the form of a brief letter to the "Editor of the American Hebrew," first of all admitting that he "hurriedly" read the invitation to contribute and then lost it. The ensuing few paragraphs, frankly, seem to have been written even more hurriedly. In answer to the question about the role of Church teaching in contemporary anti-semitism, Twain tried to make a distinction between ancient events that have lost their power to excite and ancient prejudices that nevertheless still retain vast power to sway. "It is opposed to common sense," but that has not weakened the prejudice, Twain points out. His writing here is unclear, confused, and redolent of tangents.

The next paragraph, however, anticipates a major theme of "Concerning the Jews" in thought and even in some terminology. Twain avers that the Jews do not work with their hands, only with their brains, and the "Israelites" are the only race to do so. Then:

> Is there a race that takes care of all of its poor, and suffers none to perish for want of food and shelter? Only one – the Israelites. The love of the members of an Israelitish family for each other is so strong that it amounts to devotion. Social intercourse among the Israelites is notably warm and affectionate, and but little obstructed by chilling conventions and formalities.
>
> These striking facts show the presence of the sort of qualities which civilized folk customarily admire and approve.... (Tuckey, "Fables", 447)

The letter is dated simply "March".

Years later, a week after the death of Mark Twain, in a way of acknowledging the passing of the famous author, a brief article appeared in the *American Hebrew* on April 29, 1910, headlined, "Mark Twain and the Jews." It relates that in the spring of 1890 the *Hebrew* had invited Twain to contribute to a "special number" on the subject of "the Jewish question." The journal states that it had received his answer too late for publication at the time. But the answer was not a statement; rather, it was an excuse of why he did not contribute:

To The American Hebrew: March 21st, 1890

> You sent me some questions to answer, a week or two ago, and now I don't know whether to thank you or get the police after you [presumably because the invitation diverted him from other projects]! I lost the questions, but not the topic – that will not down. It mulls and grinds through my head, all the time and obstructs and bothers work which I *must* do. Some day – I cannot tell how far, how very far away – I shall find a chance to steal a day, and then I shall satisfy myself by writing a chapter, even though it be not worth printing after it is written.
>
> Truly yours
>
> S.L. Clemens

Mark Twain might have sent a polite, curt refusal, but didn't. This letter has the aura of honesty. I would venture the guess that when he reread the statement he had hurriedly written, the text that Tuckey finally published, Twain wisely saw that it was badly composed, simplistic, and generally not worthy of a serious subject. So he never sent it, and sent in the excuses above for not contributing. While the *Hebrew's* invitation in 1890 did awaken a consideration of the Jewish question, he was not ready for it. What he needed was a catalyst to inspire him to tackle the subject. That catalyst came at the Reichsrat session in Vienna in 1897 which he described in "Stirring Times in Austria."

"Stirring Times in Austria" (published March 1898) certainly had stirred up certain readers. In his introductory paragraphs to its sequel, "Concerning the Jews," Mark Twain reports one consequence: he received many letters of a general nature from American Jews about the Jewish question, but it was one letter that inspired him to undertake a project for which, to be frank, he was not fitted: The letter-writer asked Twain why anti-Semitism still exists, whether American Jews can alleviate the condition in the United States and elsewhere, and, finally,

"Will it ever come to an end?" Well-read as he was, Mark Twain had not researched the shelves of writings on the phenomenon of anti-Semitism, and his experience was, indeed, relatively meager regarding the European-wide condition of the Jews. Obviously, though, the Jews in his Mittel Europa period had made a deeply felt impression upon him, and he obviously had been doing some wondering about them. The heated moment had come to put into writing his impression of the Jewish race that he had been asked for by the *American Hebrew* in 1890. Perhaps more important than the factual depth of his knowledge, his status as a famous American writer to this day gives continuous interest to this expression of his views on the subject.

Dolmetsch thinks that the purported letter from the American Jew was a spurious reason for writing "Concerning the Jews" anyway. A disturbing phenomenon had developed in the Viennese media concerning Mark Twain. He was becoming vilified as a Jew-lover and even as a Jew, in both printed columns and caricature replete with hooked nose that James Russell Lowell had noted. Twain's daughter, Clara, in her biography *My Father, Mark Twain* (1931) recalls that in Vienna "there were certainly evidences of much jealousy on the part of Christians, and particularly of Catholics.... Father always grew eloquent in defense of Christ's race [the Jews]. Indeed, so often were his remarks on the subject quoted that it was often rumored at one time Father himself was a Jew." *Kikeriki,* an anti-Semitic weekly, concluded that Mark Twain was a Jew because "Samuel" is an Old Testament name and the proper pronunciation of his middle name as Länghorne proves he is Jewish.[3] Twain's notebook jottings preceding the actual writing of the essay indicate that it is, in Dolmetsch's words, the "author's riposte to slanders laid upon him in the anti-Semitic Viennese press, not an impromptu reply to questions in a letter from an American lawyer."[4] Whatever the motivation, this essay is Mark Twain's climactic statement of his thoughts about the Jewish people.

First, Mark Twain clears the decks, so to speak. He emphasizes that he is untainted by prejudice, and, as proof, claims that "there was no uncourteous reference to [the Jewish] people in my books,"[5] which a friend of his had verified years earlier. Nevertheless, certain terms he had used, like "Isaac" or "Israelite" as racial nomenclature, resound with some disrespect. So his claim is not entirely true, but true enough to pass, to use Twainian terminology. Next, he outlines six topics that the essay will address, but his categories are far from strictly observed. Themes intersperse themselves under other themes, and seeming contradictions slip in. Actually, his operative ideas can be subsumed under two motifs: the justice of accusing the (racial) Jew of money-obsession with attendant enviable success, and how the Jews might guard themselves against the popular reaction to this indestructible reputation.

The Lust-for-Lucre Myth

By the end of the 19th century, the myth of Jewish wealth was centuries old, and "Mark Twain, who believed it, was…a typical uninformed gentile," asserts Jane Smith.[6] His misinformation can readily be seen in a remark he made while lauding the Jews for communal philanthropy. He states briefly that he knew of no Jews who were beggars or downtrodden workers – of course, a myopic claim for which modern readers show impatience.[7] Yet it is a compliment that the Jews' love of money did not prevent them from using some of it generously.

Nevertheless, the age-old canard that money-lust is an innate characteristic of the Jewish race led Sander Gilman, who alleged that Twain believed in Jewish diseases as a result of their rejection of Jesus as God, son of God, and/or Redeemer, to aver succinctly that, by the time Mark Twain wrote "Concerning the Jews," he believed that "The Jews are diseased, but their infection is the desire for capital."[8] The switch from actual physical disease in *Innocents Abroad* to a mental obsession sounds insightful, but no text of Twain's connects the two afflictions, probably because he saw both afflictions as part of a larger, interracial environment – *all* the downtrodden in the Holy Land suffered physical disease, not only the Jews; and *all* civilized mankind suffer the metaphorical hunger for money, not only the Jews. For him, it was axiomatic that the Jews are merely a representative – albeit collectively the most successful – of the lust-for-lucre epidemic among the damned human race, even Americans, one of whom was Mark

Twain. Back in 1872, he had penned a sketch for the Hartford *Express,* in which he imagines that he went to the revenue office and mouthed "lie after lie, fraud after fraud, villainy after villainy…But what of it? It is nothing more than thousands of the richest and proudest, and most respected, honored, and courted men in America do every year."[9] Two years before he wrote "Concerning the Jews," he reiterates the proposition that financial deviousness is not a monopoly of any one people in the following analysis:

> Consider the Dollar. The world seems to think that the love of money is "American" [not, we might note with surprise, "Jewish"!]; and that the mad desire to get suddenly rich is "American" [again, not Jewish!]. I believe that both these things are merely and broadly human, not American monopolies [or Jewish] at all. The love of money is natural to all nations, for money is a good and strong friend. I think that this love has existed everywhere, ever since the Bible called it the root of all evil.[10]

Universalizing the desire out of the narrow prejudice may theoretically compromise the anti-Jewish myth of monetary voraciousness, but it didn't help to allay persecution of the Jews because of the myth. To that phenomenon, Mark Twain pays particular attention throughout "Concerning the Jews."

In the world of commerce, Twain propounds, "The basis of successful business is honesty; a business cannot thrive where the parties to it cannot trust each other," and he claims that history awards the Jews with that trait of business honesty ("CJ", 238)! To support this surprising assertion, he brings two proofs: In past history, the Hessian Duke who had rented soldiers to England's George III for the War of American Independence, eventually had to flee his country from the advancing French Army. So he deposited $9,000,000 dollars for safe-keeping with Rothschild of Frankfurt. When the duke returned, Twain reports, "The Jew returned the loan, with interest added" ("CJ", 239). In his own times, Twain was aware that some Jews rose to be near-monopolists, but they reached that status because of their traits of honesty:

In the manner of numbers the Jew counts for little in the over-whelming population of New York; but that his honesty counts for much is guaranteed by the fact that the immense wholesale business of Broadway, from the Battery to Union Square, is sub-stantially in his hands." ("CJ", 239)

For some scholars, like Andrea Greenbaum, as we noted in an earlier chapter, even mentioning this circumstance, though laudatory, was an example of "anti-semitic" discourse.

In a reach for empirical balance, Twain admits that "The Jew has his other side. He has some discreditable ways, though he has not a monopoly of them – small forms of cheating, oppressive usury, burning himself out of business to get the insurance, "cunning con-tracts" that go only his way ("CJ", 239). Speaking of monopolies, Twain views the Jewish monopoly, with its instances of shady dealings, on Broadway as but a small-scale episode compared to the greatest Jew-ish monopoly of all time – Joseph's governance in Egypt as recounted in the Bible. Twain's perception of Joseph's acuity this time creates an unaccountable contradiction.

Again, as in *The Inncocents Abroad*, Jewish history begins for Mark Twain in the Bible. He never forgot the effect of those two Jew-ish boys of prejudiced Hannibal a half-century ago, around whom was the mystique of the ancient land of the Pharaohs, as taught in his fundamentalist Sunday school. In *The Innocents Abroad*, his por-trait of Joseph, Jewish viceroy in Pharonic Egypt, was climaxed by the awesome statement that " Joseph is one of the truly great men of the Old Testament. And he was the noblest and manliest, save Esau." (*Innocents Abroad*, 535–6). Now, decades later, Mark Twain perceives Joseph, whom he calls "the foreign Jew," quite differently:

[Joseph] made a corner in broken hearts and the crusts of the poor, and human liberty – a corner whereby he took a nation's money away, to the last penny; took a nation's livestock away, to the last hoof; took a nation's land away, to the last acre; then took the nation itself, buying it for bread, man by man, woman by woman, child by child, till all were slaves, a corner which took everything and left nothing….("CJ", 240)

Herbert L. Stewart, in 1935, crafted a defense of Joseph against these allegations: Joseph preplanned the take-over so that commodity prices would not rise, gave loans on livestock and acreage like any modern mortgage bank, and helped the farmers help themselves. Compared to the demands made upon feudal farmers of the Middle Ages by their overlords and upon southern slaves by their owners, Stewart says, Egyptian farmers were lucky.[11] But Mark Twain was not that historical; none of this entered his mind.

Furthermore, in his analysis of the causes of anti-Semitism, Mark Twain adds a searching question to conclude his indictment of Joseph:

Was Joseph establishing a character for his race which would survive long in Egypt? and in time would his name come to be familiarly used to express the character – like Shylock's? It is hardly to be doubted. ("CJ" 240)

In other words, Is Joseph a representative of the Jewish race in the same manner as Shylock is taken to be? It was almost habitual for Mark Twain to invoke the figure of Shylock when talking about financial power (as when he endowed his gentile creditor with that designation), but rarely did he point to Shylock's Jewishness. Even in the face of Bret Harte's avidity in taking loans not ever paid back, Twain did not invoke this financial misdemeanor as a sign of his being Jewish. The evocation of Shylock here, the comparison between an imagined figure and a historical one, rose up, I suggest, out of Mark Twain's memory of a debate in 1882 in the *Century* magazine, one of America's popular magazines (whose editor a year later was bowdlerizing *Huckleberry Finn* prior to publishing the novel in serial).[12] George Brandes had published a book in 1880 about Lord Beaconsfield, i.e., Benjamin Disraeli, a converted Jew who largely ignored the conversion. In it Brandes concluded that Disraeli lacked idealism but had the persistence, industry, pragmatism, wit, and ambition "of his race." Therefore, he was a "typical representative" Jew. James Bryce, a member of the British Parliament, followed with an article, "Lord Beaconsfield," in the *Century* (March 1882), which echoed Brandes's thesis. Bryce found "three...characteristics of [Disraeli's] race in full measure – detachment, intensity, scorn."

The American-Jewish poet, Emma Lazarus, annoyed by intimations that Disraeli was a kind of "Shylock" wrote a scathing response, "Was Lord Beaconsfield a Representative Jew?", published in the April 1882 issue of the *Century*. Her strategy was to offer a different tandem of imaginative and historical balance. She compared the characteristics of Disraeli and of Shylock with those of Spinoza to show that there is no such thing as representatives of the Jewish race. Each Jew is to be judged on his own. And here, Mark Twain, in 1898/9, was still implying that Joseph in Egypt established the typicality of the Jew as a cruel money-grasper, a canard that has been carried down through 3,000 years, stigmatizing Joseph himself and all Jews as companions in typicality of the unfortunate Shylock, the "oppressive" usurer. Indeed, as Twain noted years before regarding the natives of Hawaii, prejudices instilled early can never be entirely erased, proved now as a boomeranged observation.

At the same time, on the other hand, he lightens the stigma. About the connection between the financial acuity of the Jew and the indictment of usury, Twain writes an eloquent version of the well-known historical apologia for the Jews' choice of profession:

> Trade after trade was taken from the Jew by statute till practically none was left. He was forbidden to engage in agriculture; he was forbidden to practice law; he was forbidden to practice medicine, except among Jews; he was forbidden the handicrafts. Even the seats of learning and the schools of science had to be closed against this tremendous antagonist. Still, almost bereft of employments, he found ways to make money, even ways to get rich. Also ways to invest his takings well, for usury was not denied him. ("CJ", 242)

We must take note that this passage is not in a dry review of history.

Mark Twain utilized the rhetorical tactic of periodic repetition to indicate that he is not merely explanatory, he is angry, but not with the Jew, however. In his next paragraph he recalls that Protestants and Catholics have persecuted each other, yes, "but they never closed agriculture or handicrafts against [the other]," only against the Jewish minority. It is, then, clearly not a question of religious persecution, or protection against the Jews' racial ravenousness. It is mainly fear of the Jew's brain ("CJ", 242).

Concerning Christian Incompetence

What seems clear to Mark Twain is that the admitted Jewish superiority and cunning clearly take advantage to the point of victimization of their less competent rivals and competitors in business. In Mark Twain's eyes, the ineffectual victim was the Christian rival of the Jew. In that letter to Twitchell referred to above, he placed three Jews and ten Christians on the scale, and the scale tipped toward the Jews. That this a natural fact, and the Jews are not to be blamed for it, is the sum of Mark Twain's belief.

First off, he feels "convinced that the Crucifixion has not much to do [anymore] with the world's attitude towards the Jew.... I'm persuaded that in Russia, Austria, and Germany nine-tenths of the hostility to the Jew comes from the average Christian's inability to compete successfully with the average Jew in business – in either straight business or the questionable sort." Twain informs us that what led him to that conclusion is a speech he had read by a Berlin lawyer – presumably intelligent and discriminating – wherein the speaker claimed that

> In Berlin the banks, the newspapers, the theaters, the great mercantile, shipping, mining, and manufacturing interests, the big army and city contracts, the tramways, and pretty much all the other properties of high value, and *also* small businesses were in the hands of the Jews. ("CJ", 243)

Twain gives us a set of statistics, as he understood the figures presented in that speech: out of a population of 48 million, there are "only" 500 thousand Jews, but 85% of the "successful lawyers" in Berlin are Jewish. That is to say, "85% of the brains and honesty of the whole was lodged in the Jews." "Isn't it an amazing confession? …. You note the crucial point…. the argument [Mark Twain emphasizes] is that the Christian cannot *compete* with the Jew" ("CJ", 243; Twain's italics). Thirty-five years later, Herbert Stewart recast Twain's conclusion into an even more startling, way: "…A truly amazing acknowledgment of collapse on the part of 99 per cent. in conflict with 1 per cent. of the population."[13]

Twain appears to consider the inferiority of the Christians not only natural but even immutable. It must have been somewhat frustrating to ponder upon the ostensible natural inferiority of his fellow Christians (as unorthodox a Christian as Mark Twain was) and not be able to envision an amelioration of their status as underdog. Rather than accusing Mark Twain of being anti-Semitic in "Concerning the Jews" by recounting their racial faults, one can make a case that he was anti-Christian, and as we shall see, he was not unmindful that his essay can be read that way!

Advice to the Perplexed

He has no advice to offer the Christians. He says nothing to them. Twain does not laud the Christian for not being a money-getter; he does not praise their inferiority as a higher standard of morality. He does not take the opportunity to advise them to stop depending upon priests and rulers to protect them from the Jews by exiling them – as the Berlin pundit proposed for their protection ("CJ", 243). He does not even encourage his gentile readers to pick themselves up by the bootstraps and compete, because he evidently believes they cannot.

To the Jews, however, he does offer advice about how to deal with imperturbable anti-Semitism. But first, what he does not suggest is perhaps more significant than what he does advise. Twain does not call upon the Jews at all to curtail their natural braininess or their business acumen, or to ease off on the Christian's natural incapacity. And, nowhere does Twain suggest that the Jew can escape anti-Semitism by assimilating himself into the host community. The Viennese and Prague shock experiences taught him the futility of this policy. It is difficult to understand Carl Dolmetsch's suggestion that "most of the Clemens family's Jewish friends and acquaintances in Vienna were assimilationists, and it is their views Mark Twain seems to have accepted and espoused, with some reservations, when he came to write 'Concerning the Jews.'"[14] His assimilated friends in Vienna were not immune to anti-Semitism, as the vituperations on the floor in the Reichsrat and the malice of a significant section of the press prove, nor the modernist Jews of Prague who suffered in the riots that dismayed Twain.

Indeed, his advice to the Jews is vastly otherwise. He advises the Jews, in effect, to accept the inexorable situation of Christian fear and hatred, but compensate for it by organizing themselves. He urges the Jews not to hesitate to identify themselves as Jews on the censuses of the countries they reside in, thus advertising their potential political strength. He maintains that the Jews have enough numerical strength, though they are a minority, to make a difference. He offers the Irish in America to illustrate what he means: the Irish may be disliked or even feared, but they protect themselves from the effects of this situation by organizing themselves into pockets of political power. "The Irish would govern the Kingdom of Heaven if they had a strength there like that [of the Jews in Vienna]" ("CJ", 245).

Twain does not mean that the Jews should aim for political office necessarily, but to be the gray eminence behind the politicos. Everywhere, "The Jews are active in politics.... but they scatter their work and their votes among the numerous parties, and thus lose the advantages to be had by concentration" ("CJ", 247–8). Organization! Concentration! Twain trumpets, this is the key to protection from the fears and prejudices of the host majority.

This proposition sounds feasible in individual countries where a semblance of democracy exists in the political make-up. But in the case of a proposed international ingathering of Jewish power, Mark Twain hesitates. His hesitation simmers in a passage in "Concerning the Jews" regarding his friend Theodor Herzl's Zionism:

Speaking of concentration [he wrote], Dr. Herzl has a clear insight into the value of that. Have you heard of his plan? He wishes to gather the Jews of the world together in Palestine, with a government of their own – under the suzerainty of the Sultan, I suppose. At the Convention of Berne [a minor error: it was at Basle], last year, there were delegates from everywhere, and the proposal was received with decided favor. I am not the Sultan and I am not objecting; but if that concentration of the cunningest brains in the world was going to be made in a free country (bar Scotland), I think it would be politic to stop it. It will not be well to let that race find out its strength. If the horses knew theirs, we should not ride anymore. ("CJ", 248)

Highly complimentary, but perplexing. What he suggested in one breath, he retracts in another. To take Twain's advice to the Sultan seriously is to negate all the previous advice to the Jews to organize. He seems to be warning the higher political authorities everywhere to beware of Jews contemplating organized political action, indeed to act against it. If so, then all his advice to emulate the Irish is disingenuous, to say the least. It will not lead to protection against anti-Semitism. This passage probably led Dolmetsch to assert that Mark Twain "was a firm assimilationist.... unsympathetic, even derisive, toward Theodore Herzl's Zionism."[15] If there is derision here, it is of the silent sort: Mark Twain inwardly wondered how Herzl could make the idea come about, no matter how much the Jews may will it. He had seen Palestine, and that was enough.

My own opinion is that Mark Twain's sense of humor went awry at this point in his essay. Probably feeling at this late juncture of his essay that his positive feelings for Jews *as Jews* are loud and clear, he could indulge in a bit of jesting, especially in a situation upon which he can have no influence. The sure instinct that Artemus Ward instilled in him left him for the moment (note the inelegant analogy at the end of the passage!). This passage has resulted in consternation among readers ever since its publication.

A few paragraphs after this advice to the Sultan of Turkey, Twain's conclusion to "Concerning the Jews" has him swinging once again to positive perceptions of the race:

> You were the favorites of Heaven originally, and your manifold and unfair prosperities convince me that you have crowded back into that snug place again [another cynical-sounding jest, this time against heaven, not the Jews].... If the statistics are right, the Jews constitute but *one per cent* of the human race.... Properly the Jew ought hardly to be heard of; but he is heard of, has always been heard of. ("cj", 248–9)

Twain intersperses here references to the Jew's contributions to science, art, finance, medicine "away out of proportion to the weakness of his numbers." Then he surveys the grand history of the ancient empires – Egyptian, Babylonian, Roman, etc.

> The Jew saw them all, beat them all, and is now what he always was, exhibiting no decadence, no infirmities of age, no weakening of his parts, no slowing of his energies, no dulling of his alert and aggressive mind. All things are mortal but the Jew; all other forces pass, but he remains. What is the secret of his immortality? ("cj", 249).

These are the last words of "Concerning the Jews." Nineteenth-century answers to this question, as Sander Gilman reports them, include their intra-communal philanthropy, a "common mental construction," "not intermarrying with other races" – generally, "Group dynamics and racial purity are the source of Jewish health such as it is."[16] A grudging comment, perhaps, but a good generalization. Basically, it is the quality of Jewish racial consistency, that very quality Mark Twain had derogated 13 years earlier in his essay on that topic. The shock treatment in Vienna surely drove him to a new perspective.

A century later, an uncanny echo and summary of "Concerning the Jews" was intoned by a Russian-Jewish woman, director of the Riga Jewish community center in Latvia, who might not have ever heard of Mark Twain, or if she had, might never have read his essay: "'Anti-semitism is forever [she said]. Many people have envy, they say Jews have a better life. If you have money, you're bad.' And yet,…the Jews survive…. Where are the pharaohs, fascists, communists? The Jews are still here. Why is this? I can't explain it, it's on the inside, on the genetic level.'"[17]

The Aftermath

Between completing the manuscript and the publication of it, Mark Twain reacted to it in a letter of July 26, 1898, to H.H. Rogers in the States:

> The Jew article [notice the Hannibal-tone language] is my "gem of the ocean." I have taken a world of pleasure in writing it and doctoring it and fussing at it. Neither Jew nor Christians will approve of it, but people who are neither Jew *nor* Christian will, for they are in a condition to know the truth when they see it.[18]

One wonders who in the western world is neither a Christian or a Jew. Mohammedans, whom he despised? Or, is Twain referring to the doubters, like himself, in both camps, who are more objective in their views of religion and religious bodies? Nevertheless, elsewhere in this letter, he confirms that "Concerning the Jews" radiates more anti-Christian sentiments than anti-Jewish feelings:

> If I have any leaning, it is toward the Jew, not the Christian. (There is one thing I'd like to say, but I dasn't: Christianity has deluged the world with blood and tears – Judaism has caused neither for religion's sake.)[19]

Deeper down Mark Twain had a greater respect for his essay than referring to it as "the Jew article" would indicate. Privately, in his Notebook – not in his letter to a personal friend like Rogers – , he refers to it by its title. Perhaps he was afraid that Rogers might think he had lost some of his old crustiness about all religions.

Moreover, he evidently felt that this effort had more lasting significance than the ephemeral essays he had contributed over the years, and was placing, even now, in magazines. Twain instructed Rogers to place "Concerning the Jews" in *Harper's* in New York, if possible, an old repository of his work. But, as he wrote to Rogers, he was annoyed that Henry Olden, the editor of *Harper's*, downgraded its importance by calling "the Jew article 'timely' (in the sense of fresh and new *and* immediate and large interest [not in itself, but] because of the Dreyfus matter, [and therefore] wants to pay only half-price." This, Mark Twain could not accept. To him, "Concerning the Jews" had a transcendent importance beyond the Dreyfus Affair. From his wonder about the longevity of the Jewish race, we can conjecture that he had reasoned that the Dreyfus business will be resolved one day, one way or another, but the Jewish question – probably never. He cannot fathom editor Alden's comparison of this article with a minor piece called "Mental Telepathy," for which he had received half-fee: that piece was on a tired topic, Twain feels, and, besides, it was published eight years before. Finally, Twain prevailed. He got $500 for "Concerning the Jews," more than for any of the other essays in negotiation in July 1898.[20]

"Concerning the Jews" was published in *Harper's* in September 1899. Jewish reactions were soon reverberating. Just one month later, in the *Overland Monthly* of San Francisco, Bret Harte's old publication, appeared a stinging rebuke from Rabbi M.S. Levy, entitled "A Rabbi's Reply to Mark Twain." Levy makes two points: In "Concerning the Jew" Mark Twain had remarked that the Jew as citizen "is charged with the unpatriotic disinclination to stand by the flag as a soldier – like the Christian Quaker." (Levy was referring to a passage in "cj", 240.) Levy indignantly claims that the Jews in America were in the thick of the struggle against England before and during the War of Independence, mentioning the financial contribution of Hyam Solomon, and they were military heroes of the Civil War. The other point that engaged Levy's displeasure is Twain's remark about the "fat wealth of Jews." Here Levy lists eleven American monopolists and manipulators, all non-Jewish who also have acquired fat wealth.[21] A generation or two later, Louis Harap complains, that for one who wrote "a searing picture of commercial venality and rapacity – in which no Jews were involved – in his own *Gilded Age*," Twain should have known better and expressed himself more fairly.[22]

Rabbi Levy was not the only American reader annoyed by Twain's misconception about the pacifist posture of Jews. Simon Wolf, an American-Jewish historian who had published a book on *The American Jew as Patriot, Soldier, and Citizen,* straightened Twain out on this point. In response, Twain promised to write a postscript correcting his grievous error. That he did in 1904 as a "Postscript – THE JEW AS A SOLDIER," admitting that he was "ignorant" of the truth and apologized with statistics to show to what extent he was wrong. The postscript quotes Major-General O.O. Howard's testimony that soldiers of "Hebrew origin" "were the bravest and the best."[23] Almost all subsequent reprintings of "Concerning the Jews" carry this "postscript."

On October 6, 1899, a month after "Concerning the Jews" had been published in *Harper's, The American Hebrew* published an article entitled "Mark Twain Writes his Chapter." The piece is apparently a reprinted article from the *Hartford Courant,* one of Mark Twain's home-towns. It reprints Twain's letter of 1890 to the *Hebrew* explaining why he cannot respond to its invitation to write on the subject of anti-Semitism, and declares that Twain's recent essay in *Harper's* is the "chapter" he said he would write one day and had now been published.

The major intention of the *Courant* article was not an analysis of "Concerning the Jews," but a critique of Cyrus Sulzberger's response to the essay in the *American Hebrew.* Sulzberger had acknowledged Mark Twain's "spirit of absolute fairness," but objected strongly to Twain's theory that religion no longer played any part in modern anti-Semitism. Twain is all wrong, opined Sulzberger, when he attributes the lust-for-lucre, symbolized by what the *Courant* calls the "Joseph of Egypt and Shylock of Venice likeness," as the cause of contemporaneous anti-Jewishness. Rather, asserted Sulzberger, "the teachings of the Christian Church" that the Jews are Christ-killers still bears bitter fruit. The *Courant* heartily disagrees. It contends that no Christian theologian utters that indictment anymore, and quotes a statement by a Christian divine that lauds the Jewish race as evidence that that ancient accusation no longer applies.

However, it does agree with Sulzberger's opinion that Twain's advice to the Jews to identify themselves and organize politically is a terrible piece of advice. The *Courant* quotes Sulzberger: "'Were the Jews to segregate themselves in the way suggested, they would afford an easy means to their own extermination.'" As a masterpiece of unwitting erroneous prophecy, the *Courant* crows: "That's putting it much too strongly, of course; there's no possible question of extermination in the case."[24] No further comment on the *Courant's* thinking is, I think, necessary.

On the other side of the Atlantic, equally sensitive to the nuances of "Concerning the Jews," the *Jewish Chronicle* of London reacted to "Concerning the Jews" by praying, "Of all such advocates, we can but say 'Heaven save us from our friends,'" in the face of the stereotypical ideas and thin history in the essay.[25] But the *Chronicle*, like Sulzberger, did comment upon Twain's good intentions. Misdirected, misguided, narrowly educated on this subject, Mark Twain was still, after all, a friend.

The ensuing decades were rather silent about "Concerning the Jews". It was reprinted in 1900, in the collection under the title, *The Man that Corrupted Hadleyburg*." In 1928, this collection was reprinted under the copyright of Twain's daughter Clara, but the essay was not included, in all probability because Albert Bigelow Paine, Mark Twain's authorized biographer and literary executor at the time, shifted it to the collection *In Defense of Harriet Shelley* and it continues to reappear in subsequent reprintings of that collection. This bibliographical fact, ordinarily of interest only to cataloguers in the back rooms of libraries, was used in an entirely outrageous manner. Ironically, it involves the country that Mark Twain had admired during his visits to Europe, Germany. Hitler had come to power in 1933, and the world was slowly becoming aware of the as-yet "minor" atrocities committed against the Jews of Germany. In his article "Mark Twain on the Jewish Problem", published in 1935, Herbert L. Stewart already was able to compare the Berlin speech that Mark Twain had summarized 37 years earlier in "Concerning the Jews" to what "might have come from a Nazi organ of two years ago."[26]

That "Concerning the Jews" was not reprinted in Clara's collection was a fact used by a Nazi-oriented American writer in 1939 to claim that the essay was withheld because it is really anti-Jewish. To support that contention, the author offered carefully scissored and re-written passages of the essay. No less a personality than the eminent Bernard de Voto, the famous and devoted successor to Albert Bigelow Paine as literary editor of Mark Twain's writings, took up verbal cudgels to combat this outrage. He published his remonstrance in an Anglo-Jewish publication, *The Jewish Frontier*. De Voto's opening announces the problem:

> Under the title of "'Jewish Persecution' A Business Passion – Mark Twain," a leaflet is being circulated, ostensibly by one Robert Edward Edmonson,…It is based on excerpts of an essay by Mark Twain called "Concerning the Jews." A vile and dishonest misrepresentation of that essay, it is as vicious a bit of propaganda as I have ever seen….

DeVoto goes on to synopsize Twain's essay, referring mainly to that Berlin lawyer's speech and Mark Twain's advice to the Jews to organize politically. His overall opinion about "Concerning the Jews" is that "it is not a very searching analysis, but certainly it is extremely favorable to the Jews." In De Voto's judgment, Mark Twain was basically pro-Jewish: "Mark Twain's essential point…was his conviction that the Jews are the most intelligent people in the world…[The essay] is a warmhearted expression of Mark Twain's lifelong liking and admiration for the Jews." Edmonson's leaflet, he declares, "has completely perverted it," and he urges all who wish to learn the truth about Mark Twain's stance to read "Concerning the Jews" itself.[27]

It is certain that De Voto's reputation and stature would have ensured the publication of his remonstrance in a more widely read journal or newspaper. Perhaps it is a pity he did not do so. It might have lowered the decibels of the later debate about Twain's anti-Semitism. On the other hand, on the eve of the Second World War, publishing his shattering critique of a Jew-hater's dishonesty in an Anglo-Jewish, limited-circulation organ, was a gesture to the American Jewish community to remind them that the great Mark Twain – and his well-known disciple – were decidedly on their side.

Notwithstanding, "Concerning the Jews" remained controversial. In 1954, John J. Appel, an historian of American Jewry, in another Anglo-Jewish publication, *Congress Weekly*, reiterates the criticism published a half-century earlier in *The Overland Monthly* and *The Jewish Chronicle*: "Sympathy and tolerance alone, which Mark Twain…possessed in abundance, remain admirable qualities, but do not extend insight into the basic problems of intergroup understanding and amity."[28] A much stronger dissent is Jude Nixon's in *The Mark Twain Encyclopedia*: "Patronizing comments and excess [in "Concerning the Jews" are] so laced with stereotypes that the essay might appear more anti-Semitic than a defense."[29] Years have gone by since these reactions were published, but "Concerning the Jews" still rankles at least one eminent American – Jewish writer, Cynthia Ozick. As recently as 1995, she complains in *Commentary* magazine, "Mythology, it develops, is the heart and muscle of Mark Twain's reputedly 'philo-Semitic' essay – the old myths trotted out for an airing in the American idiom."[30]

These latter comments, I suggest, reflect post-Holocaust frustration and sensitivity that, in truth, the "Jewish Question" has not been answered, not in 1899 nor thereafter. However, in the climate of pseudo-scientific and authoritative "proofs" prevalent in its day that the Jews are a blot on civilization's escutcheon, "Concerning the Jews" was a brave analysis. There can be no doubt that Mark Twain's two years in Vienna was a turning-point in his perspective of the Jewish race. His allusions to Dreyfus, his reporting the hate-filled atmosphere in which the Jews of Austria-Hungary live, and the very undertaking to write on the subject of anti- Semitism show a much more serious and consciously sympathetic approach to a theme that has vexed his mind since boyhood. His admiration for the people is clear, their history is to him amazing and unique.

Verbal winking of the eye, sly humor at the expense of the Jews – sometimes misdirected – still appears; unfavorable myths he should have shucked off by now still are alluded to. That his conversion was not complete as yet in 1898 is equally clear in the two-sided responses that "Concerning the Jews" aroused intermittently for a hundred years and more. Does he ever recover entirely from the Hannibal syndrome? Perhaps the next chapter will provide an answer to that question.

Chapter Nine

TWO FANTASIES AND A
TWICE-TOLD TALE

ONE MIGHT HAVE THOUGHT that the writing of "Concerning the Jews" would have exhausted Mark Twain's interest in the Jewish race. After all, in that essay he surveyed the history of the Jews, identified what he thought was the current nature of anti-Semitism, and even offered the race a stratagem of defense – quite enough, it would seem, for a non-Jew's analysis of an ages-old cancer of Western civilization. But, no: in his last decade, Mark Twain, for the first time, introduced Jewish characters into final fictions – two fantasies and a tale he told twice. Only one of these fictions was published before his death.

Christian and Jew in Heaven

The title of this story is "Extract from Captain Stormfield's Visit to Heaven." It is a fantasy of souls that have left this earthly orb and are residents in or newcomers to an un-Christian heaven. It is difficult to place the story in the chronology of Twain's canon. Actually, "Stormfield" had one of the longest gestations of all of Mark Twain's works. One could reasonably date the very first inkling of the work as far back as 1866, when he sailed on the *Columbia* on the first leg of the San Francisco–New York trip. Two figures in his travel letters lay dormant in his creative mine. His notebooks of that period suggest that Capt. Edgar (Ned) Wakeman, whom he came to know well during that voyage, was a major inspiration-in-waiting for the character of Captain Stormfield – honest, bluff, hearty, friendly; and that the "Solomon" of his anecdote would join him one day. The actual drafting of the story began in 1868, was worked on in the 1870s and early 1900s, finally published in truncated form in 1907.[1] There seems to be no record of what parts were completed when. I have placed it in his last-decade writings because a version of it saw the light of print in 1907/8 in *Harper's,* and in book form in 1909. Twain lived long enough to decide on its content and to see it through the press in magazine as well as book. My own feeling is that the passages where a Jewish character appears were companions to the writing of "Concerning the Jews." That these passages were left behind in manuscript when "Stormfield" was published will be commented upon presently.

Janet Smith states that Twain intended the story for posthumous publication and the setting of the tale, a heaven in which Earth and its inhabitants count for nought, makes posthumous publication appropriate.[2] These were the years that death and bitterness ate into his soul. His beloved Suzy died in 1896, his brother Orion in 1897. Living memorials of his career soon followed – Dan de Quille of the *Territorial Enterprise* halcyon days in 1899, Charles Dudley Warner, collaborator on *The Gilded Age* in 1900, and Bret Harte in 1902. Bitterest of all, his beloved wife, confessor, and critic, Livy, passed on in 1904. It is no surprise that thoughts of death and after-life coagulated into a theme. The "Stormfield" tale displays Mark Twain's long-held displeasure with the fairy-tale placebo of a Christian heaven. He simply ignored the notion that it was all created to reward a human race that Twain progressively saw as "damned."

The story is told in first-person narration by the Captain himself, relating his experiences, surprises, and disillusionments to a youthful listening spirit. At one point, the souls that recently shed their earthly prison are flying to an ethereal registration point. Capt. Stormfield's spirit meets up with that of one Solomon Goldstein. This Jewish character is the first created by Mark Twain in his fiction. He is the precursor of but two (some critics suggest three) more in other late tales. While flying together, the personable and sociable Captain engages Goldstein in conversation:

I was trained to a prejudice against Jews [Stormfield remarks to his listener] – Christians always are you know – but such of it as I had was in my head, there wasn't any in my heart. Then [Goldstein and I] were quiet a long time, and I let him alone, and let him think. Now and then he sighed, and by and by I found he was crying. You know, I was mad with him in a minute; and says to myself, "Just like a Jew! he has promised some hayseed or other a coat for four dollars, and now he has made up his mind that if he was back [on earth in his store] he could work off a worse one on him for five. They haven't any heart – that race – nor any principles."…At last I broke out and said –

"Cheese it! Damn the coat! Drop it out of your mind."

"Goat?" [= "coat"; Goldstein speaks English with a "Yiddishic" accent]

"Yes. Find something else to cry about."

"Why I wasn't crying aboud a goat."

"What then?"

"Oh, captain, I loss my little taughter [daughter], and now I never, never see her again any more. It break my heart!"

By God, it went through me like a knife. I wouldn't feel so mean again, and so grieved, not for a fleet of ships. And I spoke out and said what I felt; and went on damning myself for a hound till he was so distressed I had to stop…. He said it was only a mistake, and a mistake wasn't a crime.

There now – wasn't it magnanimous [of Goldstein]? I ask you – wasn't it? I think so. To my mind there was the stuff in him for a Christian; and I came out flat-footed and told him so….[3]

For "Capt. Stormfield" in this passage, read "Sam Clemens/Mark Twain." The tendency of the conditioned mind to rake up the old myth of the money-voracious Jew is by now an old story in Mark Twain's canon. Here he acknowledges that this canard was instilled in him from his boyhood by adults who should have known better. Twice before Twain had obliquely anticipated the substance of this confession in two totally unrelated essays, tacit evidence that the Hannibal syndrome had bothered him for many years. In this context it is worth repeating what we have already noted above: In the 1873 sketch about the Sandwich Islands, he had observed: "[The natives'] ancient superstitions are in their blood and bones, and they keep cropping out now and then in the most natural and pardonable way,"[4] like the humorous slights about the Jews that Mark Twain occasionally slipped into his essays over the years. The other passage of self-examination and confession comes in a late essay, "Is Shakespeare Dead?", published in 1909: "When even the brightest mind in our world has been trained up from childhood to a superstition of any kind, it will never be possible for that mind, in its maturity, to examine sincerely, dispassionately, and conscientiously any evidence or any circumstance which shall seem to cast a doubt upon the validity of that superstition. I doubt if I could do it myself."[5] He tried to do so, however, with "Concerning the Jews" and the Stormfield story.

"In the scene in "Stormfield," says Carl Dolmetsch, "Solomon Goldstein…converts Stormfield from his life-long prejudice against Jews in somewhat the same way Jim confounds Huck's preconceptions about blacks."[6] Dolmetsch is referring to the end of chapter 15 of *Adventures of Huckleberry Finn*: Huck had played a trick on Jim the black slave and was put in his place by the slave who actually calls him "trash." Then, says Huck: "It was fifteen minutes before I could work myself up to go and humble myself to a nigger, but I done it, and warn't ever sorry for it afterward, neither." Both Huck and Stormfield to a large extent are alter egos for Sam Clemens. The verbal echo in "Stormfield" is dramatic, but it must also be pointed out that the matter thrusts more personally and deeply. Clemens never had a prejudice against Negroes. He did against Jews at one time in his life. The "Stormfield" passage reveals and emphasizes that Mark Twain had both the self-analytical sense to realize the thoughtlessness of his sometime attitudes, and the humility to confess it as a weakness.

It came late and hard. Janet Smith remarks that "Mark Twain was not born to tolerance: he achieved it and had it thrust upon him by experience. And perhaps that is why it ran somewhat deeper in him than the lip service which sometimes passes for that great quality."[7] Yet the ingrained prejudice evidently cannot be gotten rid of entirely. Even here, when the Stormfield tale was published in 1907/9, under the title of "An Extract from Captain Stormfield's Visit to Heaven," nurtured through the presses of magazine and book by Mark Twain himself, the Goldstein segment was omitted. We don't know why. Nor is it restored in Neider's edition of the *Collected Short Stories*. Louis Harap conjectures, "Perhaps Twain wished to avoid comment on the sensitive subject of anti-Jewish prejudice."[8] That does not seem cogent, for he had recently written "Concerning the Jews," a widely read essay on just that subject. Perhaps, having written that essay, he felt that his liberal credentials were secure, and adding anything more in that line would be protesting too much. In any case, the Stormfield-Goldstein passage was written, it was not destroyed, it waited extant for posthumous publication by Mark Twain scholars.

Enter Satan, Slyly

The gestation of *The Mysterious Stranger,* posthumously published, which contains one ostensible Jew and another suggested by a critic's interpretation, is even more confused. That Mark Twain worked on it in an era before the computer's word-processor is a wonder in itself, for there are several versions in manuscript, none completed, each showing the revisions, rewritings, "cuts-and-pastings" from one version to another. Unlike *Stormfield,* we do not have a text bearing the final decisions and imprimatur of Mark Twain himself. But one character dominates through the welter of changes in these manuscripts – Satan.

In the last 30 years scholars have published and commented upon the problems of textual purity as well as the thematic importance of what came to be known as *The Mysterious Stranger.* William M. Gibson put everything in order in *Mark Twain's Mysterious Stranger Manuscripts,* published in 1970 under the auspices of the Mark Twain Project at the University of California, Berkeley. While it is far beyond our purpose here to discuss the textual problems, there are one or two aspects that demand our attention. Perhaps the best way to approach is to have a digest of Gibson's introduction before us:

Version A – September 1897: (*Arrival in Vienna*). Originally the story was set in a town called St. Petersburg, a flimsy alias of Hannibal, Missouri. The plot involves the foreclosure by *the village bank* (note my emphasis) of the mortgage in which two sympathetic characters live. This version was amalgamated into the early chapters of –

Version B – "The Chronicle of Young Satan": November 1897–September 1900: The expanded cast of major characters include Theodor, the youthful narrator and two of his boyfriends; Father Adolf, a wicked priest; Father Peter, a good priest; Marget, his niece; Wilhelm, her swain; and, of course, Satan of the title, a rambuncious, clever, unprincipled teenager, disguised of course. Father Peter discovers a bag of gold coins, which he intends to use to pay off the mortgage on his house (see version A), held in this version, not by *the village bank,* but by *Solomon Isaacs, obviously Jewish.* The good Father Peter is accused of stealing the gold, and Satan manipulates things so that he is declared not guilty. After this plot is resolved, the manuscript then begins but breaks off in the middle of an adventure of Satan and Theodor.

It is significant that this version was formulated after Mark Twain had attended the session of the Austrian Reichsrat that resulted in "Stirring Times in Austria" and partially reworked during the months he wrote and published "Concerning the Jews."

Version C – November 1898, "Schoolhouse Hill." The notes for this story are dated June–July 1897.[9] The manuscript has the beginnings of a comic plot involving Tom Sawyer, Huck Finn, and a new boy in the school, who is "young Satan." This story was abandoned altogether, but one or two elements survived, together with the notes outlining Twain's intentions.

Version D – 1901/2, "No. 44: The Mysterious Stranger" begun. This, the longest of the manuscripts, is called the "Printer's Devil" or "Print Shop" version, because the whole central portion of the manuscript was inspired by Twain's recollections of his teenage profession. (It is in this telling of the Satanic tale that one scholar's imagination found hints of a Jewish connection with Satan; see below).

The most popular version of the four is Version B. It forms the core of the one published by Twain's literary executor, Albert Bigelow Paine, and his collaborator Franklin Duneka in 1916 that has horrified scholars when they came to studying the manuscripts. They discovered that the published tale was made up of Version B + part of Version D + a bit of characterization from Version C + their own additions and emendations. One of the "crimes" was to graft chapter 37 of Version D onto Version B as its last chapter. It fit so well, rounding out the only integrated, coherent, if uncompleted, story-line of the four versions, that no one noticed or cared until the Twain scholar John Tuckey discovered it. Paine and Duneka had named their version *The Mysterious Stranger.* This is the text reprinted by Bernard de Voto in his *Portable Mark Twain* in 1946, and again by Charles Neider in his *Complete Short Stories of Mark Twain* in 1957.

Even Tuckey, who discovered the emendations and interpolations of Paine and Duneka, came to admit that this version belongs to the people, let the scholars worry about the principle of the purity of the text. Despite Paine and Duneka's cancelling 25% of "The Chronicle," changing the *dramatist personae,* and adding a chapter, it is "the only existing form of the story that has the coherence and completeness of a realized literary form." For 50 years it has "held its place in our literature" for readers, students, and scholars. Tuckey awards it the accolade of being "the most important work of Mark Twain's later years" – "Does it deserve to perish, to endure, or to prevail?"[10] Obviously, it will prevail. In the discussion that follows, the title *The Mysterious Stranger* will refer to this well-known text.

When Mark Twain brought Version A over to B, the "Chronicle story," he naturally made certain revisions. For us in this study one revision is deeply significant: Originally, it was the village bank that held the mortgage on the house of Father Peter and his niece Marget. Now Twain revised "village bank" to read "Solomon Isaacs, money lender"[11] ("Solomon" again – Capt. Wakeman's acquaintance, Stormfield's companion!) Thus Twain not only introduced an obviously Jewish character into this tale of Austria in 1590, but also endowed him with a heretofore hated label, "money-lender." For *The Mysterious Stranger,* Twain now grafted on to "Solomon" the generic Jewish name "Isaac" from the *Alta California* letters of that long-ago voyage, to yield "Solomon Isaacs". Thirty years had gone by; this character was not forgotten, but Twain changed the disreputable characterization of his origin.

The Mysterious Stranger at first tells us that "Solomon Isaacs had lent all the money he was willing to put on the house, and gave notice that tomorrow he would foreclose."[12] On first reading, this characterization of this Jewish character as money-lender and forecloser might lead us to conclude that Twain had relapsed into the mythic slur of the heartless Jewish landlord. Not so. "Solomon Isaacs" appears twice more in this story. The next mention: After Satan stuffs Father Peter's strangely lost wallet with gold, and the honest priest is convinced by the three boys who witnessed his finding the wallet that the gold really now belongs to him, the old man "paid Solomon Isaacs [the mortgage] in gold and *left the rest of the money with him at interest* [my italics]" until, Father Peter insists, the real owner shows up.[13] Father Peter has no second thoughts about trusting Solomon Isaacs, the Jew. One is reminded of Twain's allusion in "Concerning the Jews" to the fugitive Hessian Duke who risked leaving millions with Rothschild of Frankfurt and got back his money plus interest after two years, proving that a Jew can be an honest financial agent. It would seem that Solomon Isaacs of Eseldorf, Austria, in 1590, had the same probity.

The final scene in which Solomon Isaacs appears comes after Father Adolf the villain, accuses Father Peter of stealing his gold; a trial is held, and Satan comes along to help Father Peter. He dissolves himself into Wilhelm, Marget's swain, who is serving as an ineffective defense attorney and Satan proves that Adolf is a liar. "Father Adolf went off dissatisfied and cursing and Solomon Isaacs gathered up the money and carried it away. *It was Father Peter's for good and all, now* [my italics]."[14] He did so in the courtroom in front of everybody. Not a murmur from anyone, no objection by anyone, no slur; no snicker by Mark Twain. Evidently, Solomon Isaacs enjoyed the confidence not only of Father Peter, but of the entire township of Eseldorf! *The Mysterious Stranger* actually characterizes Solomon Isaacs as a man of business, but with a kindly heart, extending the loan as long as he could, acting now as a dependable financial agent. For Twain, that is next to saintliness.

So when finally he did create a Jewish character in his fiction, Mark Twain did so without the humorous, but sticky jests, without the inherited myths of money-lust, without the supreme self-centeredness of the mythical Jew that dotted his canon from time to time. There is no need to attest to the coexistence now of two sides of the Jew in Mark Twain's mind. He is entirely favorable now.

The critic Susan Gillman suggests that there's another "Jew" in *The Mysterious Stranger* – more particularly in Version D, "No. 44: The Mysterious Stranger…." – Satan himself! But that contention needs a case to judge it: Apparently, the origin of Mark Twain's satanic persona lies somehow in recollections of Hannibal's Jewish kids. There seems to be a creative sequence, a stream of consciousness in Mark Twain's mind, traced by his notes for the story. First off, his notes tell of a "new 'Huck Finn'" tale, but immediately the notes betray a darker counterpoint. Out of the depths of old memory of more than half a century rise "the [Jewish] Lev'n boys [who] were to be suspiciously regarded by the town" and "Tom was to stand by them and have fights."[15] This time, however, the boys were to be defended, not crucified. Next, Twain intended to revise that old favorite joke about two times the Levin boys – Levin (i.e., eleven) × 2 = "Twenty-two" – by giving them new numbers, "9 and 18." But their significance is a mystery. Carl Dolmetsch remarks that some critics tried to find a cabalistic source for these numbers, but without much success.[16] Henry Nash Smith suggests that "No. 44" as the name Twain gave Satan in Version D does derive from the Levin joke: 'leven × 2 = 22, doubled again = 44. Susan Gillman interprets this numbers game as indicating Twain's judgment that Hannibal, " a slave-holding community" to begin with, now was remembered by Twain as anti-Semitic as well.[17] Finally, Kenneth Lynn interprets this suggestion as signifying that Twain, without the number shenanigans, thought of his hero as a Jew – a veritable Moses delivering the people around him to freedom.[18]

In Paine's amended form of "Chronicle of Young Satan," in addition to prankishness and showing-off, Satan attests to a bleak philosophy: human morality (the "moral sense" in version D, "No. 44...") is the bane of human existence, and Satan destroys the idealistic illusions of young Theodor. Satan also has a cynically cruel streak: he promises his friends he will make Father Peter happy and does so – by making him mad upon being acquitted at the trial, thereby separating him from reality and ensuring his continued happiness. On the other hand, Twain does portray one character as respected and trustworthy – the Jew Solomon Isaacs.

However, Gillman ignores all this when she interprets Satan as a Jew. She points out that the writing of "Chronicle of a Young Satan" is exactly simultaneous with the anti-Semitism of the *fin-de-siecle* in Europe and the display of it in Vienna. Mark Twains wrote two essays resulting from that experience. Thus, she contends, *The Mysterious Stranger* is an allied text to "Concerning the Jews." She writes that Twain saw "eternal race prejudice against the Jew as rooted in his being a 'foreigner' in the German sense – *stranger*." Furthermore, the manuscript originally named the wicked priest "Father Lueger," the name of the virulent anti-Semitic mayor of Vienna, and Twain changed it to "Father Adolf." This period of time was also the acme of the Dreyfus Affair, another proof for Twain of the persecution of the Jew,[19] as young Satan was persecuted (although for tactical reasons he never alluded to Dreyfus as such). "Satan, the fallen angel," Gillman asserts, "is the Jew, at once the persecuted, the diseased [citing Sander Gilman], and the chosen." Her interpretation comes down to an elongated equation: Satan as "persecuted innocent" = Dreyfus as "persecuted and unoffending man" $\therefore$ "virtually identified" as a Jew.[20] QED.

Her analysis is ingenious, but is not entirely convincing about the character Mark Twain created in "Chronicle of Young Satan" and "No. 44...." First, nowhere in these stories is Satan persecuted. Rather, he is the manipulator, a supreme power above all the other dramatis personae. He is charming, disarming, displaying a self-sufficiency that hasn't been characteristic of the Jew since Solomon's Temple was destroyed.

Second, in one passage of "No. 44..." Twain reprises his thesis from "Concerning the Jews" that the Jew in finance is more able than his Christian neighbor. Emil Schwarz (August – the narrator's "duplicate,") delivers a lesson in commercial history:

> The government statistics of [Constantine's] period showed that a Jew could make as much money in five days as a Christian could in six; so Constantine saw that at that rate the Jews would by and by have all the wealth [like Twain's Joseph in "Concerning the Jews"] and the Christians all the poverty.... So [Constantine] added the Sunday-Sabbath [to the Jews' Saturday – Sabbath], and it worked just right, because it equalled the prosperities. After that, the Jew had to idle 104 days in the year. the Christian only 52, and this enabled the Christian to catch up. [However,]...there was now talk among Constantine and other early Christians up there [in heaven], of some more equalizing.... Along in the twentieth century somewhere it was going to be necessary to furnish the Jews another sabbath to keep, so as to save what might be left of Christian property at that time.[21]

This does not sound like the obsequious, persecuted Jew in Gillman's characterization. Indeed, Sholom Kahn hears in these stories the Twainian "complex of philo-Semitism, sharpened by the encounter with virulent anti-Semitism in Vienna".[22]

Third, it may be that in Mark Twain's Eseldorf, Satan is a stranger, but that does not make him a Jewish character. Solomon Isaacs is a Jewish character, but he is not portrayed as a stranger. And as far as the "diseased Jew" is concerned, Gillman offers no text in these fictions where the Jew – neither Satan nor Solomon Isaacs – is described as even suffering. As in *Innocents Abroad,* there is no textual evidence that Mark Twain believed it.

Lastly, in *The Mysterious Stranger,* Satan is not the Christian or Miltonic Seducer of Man to evil and sin. In the conclusion to the story, he *is* a Seducer, but to despair, not to sin, in keeping with Mark Twain's despondent mood during the latter dark years. Man is quite efficient in sinning by himself – even priests like Father Adolf are exemplars. It is hard to imagine the author of "Concerning the Jews" creating a Jew arguing that the "moral sense" – which Mark Twain's Biblical Jews gave to Western Civilization – as a sham, a snare, a mistake. With all his misdemeanors in business, the Jew in Twain's eyes is an emblem of honesty in that essay and in *The Mysterious Stranger.* Furthermore, the old moral sense that drove Mark Twain in his classic novels is not dead. There are situations in this late tale where the "moral sense" as we know it does prevails. Nefarious Satan himself does not permit the guiltless to be judged guilty, as in the Dreyfus Case by French jurists. The wicked priest does not triumph. And there are other characters who represent Mark Twain's belief in the "moral sense" as in the days of *Huckleberry Finn.* One of them is Solomon Isaacs, the Jew.

Final Fictions: "Newhouse's / Randall's Jew Story"

Among the manuscripts unpublished in Mark Twain's lifetime dating from the period of "Concerning the Jews," that is, 1897/8 on to 1900, are two treatments of the same story about a Jew on a trip down the Mississippi. John Tuckey published the two brief tales in *Mark Twain's Fables of Man* in 1972.[23]

An anecdotal version under the title "Newhouse's Jew Story," takes all of 2½ pages. It begins autobiographically. About 1860, we are told, Sam Clemens was visiting an old Mississippi River pilot, George Newhouse, in his pilot-house when a passenger joined them and during the course of a conversation, made a "scurrilous" remark about Jews. Newhouse exiled him from the pilot house, and explained why to the surprised young Clemens. Fifteen years earlier, on a river steamer, an unscrupulous gambler named Jackson was fleecing a rich Louisiana farmer heavily, already winning away the planter's cash and slaves, and next was his daughter's black servant/companion since birth. This Jackson was notorious for challenging anyone accusing him of cheating to a duel, and winning that, too. (Dueling was honorable, in those days). The Louisianian lost the young slave, too, and no amount of pleading changed the gambler's mind. Her mistress, the loser's daughter, called Jackson a cheat and the gambler turned to her father and said, "I can't punish a child for that but I'll slap your face for it," which would, of course, have been a challenge to a duel that no doubt would have resulted in the father's death.

Suddenly, related Newhouse, an anonymous young Jew jumped between them and hit Jackson with the back of his hand on the mouth. This of course meant a duel between them. So they docked the boat, and the two duelists with their seconds went ashore with pistols. Pistol shots were heard, and (the way Newhouse told the story) only "three of the men came aboard again." Lengthy pause. Naturally, the silence of suspense was broken by young Sam Clemens, "Which one did you leave ashore?" "Newhouse gave him a satisfied grin, and said, 'Well, it wasn't the Jew'" (278).

In this version, the narrator, Newhouse, is, of course, named; so are Jackson, the gambler, and old Mr. Mason, the Louisiana planter; these are somewhat characterized. However, Mark Twain refrained from endowing "the Jew" with a name or character dimension. Only from his actions do we learn merely that he is highly self-assured.

The story seemed to itch Mark Twain's consciousness. He expanded the anecdote into a brief story, "Randall's Jew Story" (John Tuckey's title), about four pages long. This time Twain places the Jew squarely in the center of attention. He even formally introduces the tale with a headnote, surprisingly quoting in full the famous passage from Shakespeare's *Merchant of Venice* in which Shylock humanizes the Jew by querying, "Hath not a Jew eyes? hath not a Jew hands, organs, dimensions…?" This is not quite the same Shylock character that on numerous occasions served as Twain's symbol of Jewish money-hunger or usurious cruelty. Clearly, in this version of Newhouse's story, Twain's interest will not be simply the brief plot, but the character of the Jewish hero.

In the expository part of the story, a group of elderly gentlemen are discussing a subject which was "a heating one – the Jews. Clearly the Jew was well hated there" (284). At length, Mr. Randall, a banker, impelled by the tenor of the discussion (like Newhouse in the earlier version), begins to narrate a story. The setting is again shipboard, around 1850. Among the passengers, Randall, the narrator, recalls, were a professional gambler named Hackett, an old Virginian planter, Fairfax, and his daughter, and her Negro maid, Judith. Also, "there was a young Jew – Rosenthal – handsome, courteous, intelligent, alert, good-hearted, but a Jew; so, naturally I kept away from him" (285). Like Mark Twain and Captain Stormfield, Randall admits to native anti-Jewish prejudice. There's something confessional about Twain's creating characters in his old age that reflect his earlier anti-Jewish feelings.

The plot follows the same rising action as in the earlier anecdote, but two features deserve mention: Mark Twain, master story-teller, takes the time to increase suspense on the way to the climax by indulging in a bit of foreshadowing, like the statement: "[The bystanders'] sympathies were with the planter, but they did not know how to interfere, or maybe did not want to risk it" (285), anticipating the later juncture in the story when the Jew, in contrast, will risk interfering. And when he does accuse the gambler of robbing an honest man, the crook orders him to betake himself "out of danger." To which the Jew replies, "Thanks – many thanks. With your permission I will remain and sample the danger" (286). The Jew is applauded and cheered by the other kibitzers, but he stands alone. The game goes on, with no diminution of the cheating. "The Jew said, as if to himself: 'It is inhuman. By God it is fiendish. The man has no heart in his body'" (287).

At this point the scene between daughter and Negro slave-girl and gambler is enacted, as in Newhouse's earlier brief story. All present felt a "deep pity" for the young slave girl, "But the Jew went further – he *materialized* his pity – put up his money to try to save her; he had a bigger heart than those others" (288, Twain's italics). That Mark Twain, in past remarks, respected and admired Jewish intra-communal responsibility was one thing; to fashion a story in which a Jew as a disinterested human being applies it to a member of the lowest social status of the time is quite another compliment. Furthermore, it is a point of positive irony that Mark Twain, a money-lover himself, invented this gratuitous incident for a member of the race that was despised and feared for its monolithic avidity for money.

As Newhouse had related, the Jew interferes, challenges the gambler to a duel and kills him. But Mark Twain does not leave off the story without a paragraph of praise for his Jewish hero as "smart all around," "perfectly level-headed," "a very superior man." "And the finest thing of all was risking his life out of pure humanity...." (289). And, again like Stormfield, Mr. Randall concludes, "I have weighed his people ever since in scales which are not loaded" (289). "Mr. Randall" is clearly another alter-ego of "Sam Clemens."

One interpretation of these stories notes that "Both liberators are explicitly described as Jewish – the result, in all likelihood of Twain's all but automatic association of slave-liberation with the Moses story."[24] I feel that this is not likely at all. True, Randall is liberated from the enslavement to an ancient prejudice, but the Negro girl is not liberated. She remains a slave, though saved from the ugly purposes the gambler had in mind. This is not essentially a story of liberation, but of the heroism of a Jew acting uncharacteristically against all mythic beliefs to defend another human being who happened to be of a different minority race and color.

John Tuckey scientifically examined and dated the ink and the paper of the manuscripts upon which Mark Twain had written the stories and concluded that they were written anywhere between 1896 and the "'90s" (279, 283), the period of the Viennese shocks. I would like to suggest an even more limited dating that may indicate why Mark Twain wrote so glaring a tale of Jewish valor. As favorable to the Jews as "Concerning the Jews" was when published in 1899, it contained the misstatement about the Jewish pacifist tendency not to bear arms in defense of their adopted country. As reported above in chapter 8, he was straightened out on this point, and in 1904 that essay was reprinted with a "Postscript – THE JEW AS SOLDIER" as an apology. I suggest that the Newhouse/Randall stories were intended as an apology for that error, written when he was first criticized in print, that is, around 1899–1901. The post-script to "Concerning the Jews" is dated 1904.

The story was never published, possibly because he decided that the postscript was a more direct and appropriate apology. Possibly also, critical truth to tell, as stories, they are not very good, too extreme in the characterization of the Jew to be accepted as a plausible figure in a piece of fiction. Mark Twain was too intent, I suggest, upon making this Jew a nearly perfect counter-point to the pacifist idea, thereby making it counter-productive as a believable apology. Newhouse's story had clearly impressed the 25-year-old Sam Clemens, the Mark-Twain-to-be, back in 1860, but was repressed, waiting for sublimation. Late in life, he recalled that his attitude toward Jews was changed in 1860, when, he had heard the story from George Newhouse. The incident compromised for him the "cliche of the Jew as self-interested and cowardly," says Louis Harap.[25]

And yet: In "Randall's" retelling, though Twain gives a name to his hero-to-be, and even lists five positive characteristics of this Jew, he is still an alien. Never again in the story does Twain call his hero by name; nearly a dozen more times he refers to him by "the Jew." Notwithstanding a touch of individuation by naming him once, Mark Twain is still standoffishly racial.

Mark Twain critics have recognized the importance of the Newhouse/Randall sequence in the evolution of his thinking about Jews. "The unnamed Jew becomes a hero," writes Carl Dolmetsch, "when, in contrast to the moral cowardice of his fellow passengers, he challenges the unscrupulous gambler to a duel and kills him."[26] Other critics broaden the significance of remembering Newhouse's anecdote. Earl Briden features it in his article on "Dueling" in the *Mark Twain Encyclopedia,* as "satirizing anti-Semitism by dramatizing the benevolence and courage of a Jewish hero…using the code's compulsions to rid the [Mississippi] River of a dissolute gambler." For Twain, dueling was a vicious practice, but it did display "genuine strength of character and [in this instance] an attack on prejudice."[27] Shelley Fishkin sees it as part of a three-pronged attack on anti-Semitism that Mark Twain launched in these years: "Newhouse's Jew Story," "Randall's Jew Story," and "Concerning the Jews"; but Fishkin balances them with the remark that they are "clearly well-meaning, if limited, in [their] effectiveness."[28]

Judging his last literary efforts as philo-Semitic propaganda, Fishkin's hesitancy is no doubt justified, but they nevertheless do reveal a major shift in Mark Twain's own perception of the race. In these last critical years of honing his attitudes, Mark Twain's Jews advanced in his essays and creative efforts from being reported as abject victims of verbal and physical onslaughts as in "Stirring Times in Austria" (reincarnations in his mind, perhaps, of the victimized Levin boys of Hannibal). In *The Mysterious Stranger* he is a respected figure of honesty and reliability. In the "Newhouse/Randall" fragment he has become an appreciated paragon of selflessness and physical heroism.

One might even claim that Mark Twain achieved what he once thought was nigh impossible – that is, to wipe the mental slate clean of inherited and ingrained prejudices from childhood. It would seem, that in his last fictions, he revealed himself as finally cured of the ravages of the Hannibal syndrome – nearly all of them, at any rate. Lamentably, it was perhaps too late in his creative life to build great fiction around them.

Chapter Ten

ADULATION AT THE END

WHEN the 20th century dawned, "the unfortunate controversy over 'Concerning the Jews'" as Philip Foner called it, was evidently behind Mark Twain.[1] The Jews did not bow out of his life, nor he out of theirs. "In New York's teeming East Side," writes Janet Smith, "the Jewish immigrants regarded Mark Twain in the most affectionate terms, and nothing that critics of his essay said seems to have influenced their affection for him."[2] Mark Twain's Jews, once wraiths of the bible or intellectuals of Vienna, now comprised the immigrants of all classes. He felt comfortable enough in the presence of a Jewish crowd, and vice-versa, to attend a meeting of the Hebrew Technical High School for Girls at Temple Emanuel in New York on January 20, 1901, where he was introduced as a great writer who once wrote that he had no preference between black or white, Jew or Gentile – "to him all men were alike."[3] As if to exemplify his reputation as a great democrat and his new affinity to Jews quite different from the Viennese elite, in 1905 he addressed a benefit for Russian Jews – at which the legendary Sarah Bernhardt performed.[4] Memories of Adah Menken, the Jewess, in Virginia City in 1860s!

A few years later another encounter between Mark Twain and a crowd of Jews was recorded by Hamlin Garland, one of the young current writers of realistic fiction. After a performance of a dramatization of *The Prince and the Pauper* at the Educational Alliance, the Jewish community center for new immigrants on the Lower East Side of New York City, "Mark went on the stage," Garland reports, "and was instantly surrounded by a mob of black-eyed black-haired Orientals [i.e., Jews]" in adulation.[5]

The Educational Alliance was the venue of another encounter that has become more well-known. At this event, Mark Twain met the great Yiddish humorist Sholom Aleichem. This incident needs a brief historical background. Sholom Aleichem wrote in three languages, all unknown to Mark Twain: Hebrew, Russian, and far above all, Yiddish – humorous, realistic tales of East European *shtetl* Jews and *shtetl* life. To the immigrant East Side Jews, Sholom Aleichem was just one rung below the angels, endowed with the ability to put into words their thoughts, hopes, memories, tears, and laughter.

There was no English translation of his Yiddish tales until 1918, eight years after Mark Twain had died.[6] Nevertheless, when Sholom Aleichem arrived for an extended visit to New York on October 20, 1906, the *New York Times* noted it the next day under the headline, "Jewish Mark Twain Here," which no doubt caught the eye of Mark Twain. On October 22, the *Times* published an interview with the famous Yiddish writer. The headline again ranks Sholom Aleicheim with America's chief humorist: "The Jewish Mark Twain Enjoys Freedom Here," and the reporter actually opines that his work "rivals the best work of Mark Twain." (The article also added by the way that "a slight resemblance in feature [existed] to the Mark Twain of the pilot-house period." (Just somewhat unruly hair and bandit moustache, one trusts – not Semitic nose again!)

The interviewer elicited from Sholom Aleichem his favorite authors – Byron, Kipling, Shakespeare, and Mark Twain, "the greatest of whom was Mark Twain." He admired most Twain's collection of sketches that had been translated into Yiddish.[7] It is well-nigh impossible for Twain to have missed these articles in New York's most respected newspaper, and his was not a personality that would have pooh-poohed being classed with Shakespeare and even considered greater than the Bard by a writer who attracted so much admired attention in the *New York Times* of all places.

A short while later Twain was invited to a gathering at the Educational Alliance. The guest list included Jacob Schiff, Felix Warburg, Nathan Straus, and, "the pride of the American Jewish community, Judge Samuel Greenbaum, Vice-President of the Bar Association of New York and other Jewish organizations," according to Sholom Aleichem's daughter, Marie Waife-Goldberg, and Mark Twain and Sholom Aleichem. On the criteria of wealth, success, and influence, this was once Twain's preferred type of crowd. In her biography of her father, Waife-Goldberg describes the incandescent moment: "It was "Justice Greenbaum…[who] introduced my father to the great American humorist as 'the Jewish Mark Twain', to which Mark Twain graciously replied, 'Please tell him [probably assuming that Sholom Aleichem did not understand English] that I am the American Sholom Aleichem."[8] No doubt impressed by what he read in the *Times,* Mark Twain showed the ultimate courtesy – his was no tight-lipped smile of acknowledgment of an unwanted, tasteless compliment by an obsequious upstart. Here was no fear of a rival or distaste for an aggressive, "pushy" Jew. Here was genuine respect for a fellow worker in the orchard of serious humor.

A telling incident concerning Twain's activities among Jews occurred in 1908 when Twain had moved into his last home, which he called "Stormfield," near Redding, Conn. The house was burgled and the criminals caught, two youngsters. Mark Twain spoke to them. He told them that he had been on the "East Side [of New York City] working for just such fellows as you," adding gratuitously, because he was so involved, "and I made the Police Commissioner take back what he said about Jews." Upon which one youthful burglar admitted that he was Jewish. Mark Twain retorted, "Then you are a disgrace to your race."[9]

From this we learn that Mark Twain spent time in the hot-bed of Eastern European Jewish immigrants, the lower East Side of New York City, where he apparently involved himself in social work among them, even protecting them from the prejudices of the New York Police Commissioner himself. To appreciate this latter-day involvement of Mark Twain with the unassimilated, unmonied Jewish community one might contrast it with the reaction of another American writer who visited the same locale during the same period (1905), Henry James. James describes the flock of Jews thus: "There is no swarming like that of Israel when once Israel has got a start," observed James in his journal *The American Scene*, "and the scene here [Rutgers Street] bristled, at every step, with the signs and sounds, immitigable, unmistakable, of a Jewry that had burst all bounds."[10] "Swarming" is a term that Mark Twain used in one passage in "Concerning the Jews" – and Andrea Greenbaum berated him for it in her article "Mark Twain 's Anti-Semitic Discourse." Henry James uses it four times on a single page: "it was the sense of a great swarming;" "a swarming that had begun to thicken;" "there is no swarming like that of Israel;" "the children swarmed above all" (131). From the pen of a fastidious stylist like Henry James, this proximity of repetition goes beyond mere description. Unlike Mark Twain, James must have felt absolutely repelled by these uncouth, supernumerary Jews.

The "intensity" of the individual Jew as a member of his "race [which] permits chopping into myriads of fine fragments" drove Henry James to an analogy to make his point clear: "There are small animals," he writes, " known to natural history, snakes or worms, I believe, who, when cut into pieces, wriggle away contentedly and live in the snippet as completely as in the whole. So the denizens of the New York Ghetto…." (132). The choice of the images of the analogy clarifies his point about the individual Jew, and also clarifies Henry James's perceptions about the Jew as a human being.

Not only was it repulsion that affected Henry James. He felt intimidated. "…Who can ever tell, moreover, in any conditions and in presence of any apparent anomaly, what the genius of Israel may, or may not, really be 'up to'?" (135). What, shall we suppose, *can* they be up to in the land of the free and the home of the brave? A conspiracy to buy-up the federal, state, or city government? A poisoning of the water supply, like the alleged poisoning of the wells of Europe? A deliberate contagion of a social cancer in the American society? (Was his question an echo of *The Protocols of the Elders of Zion,* perpetrated on Western civilization just a few years earlier?) Perhaps it is to be expected from this scion of New England Brahmins, suffering from the myths and prejudices imbibed in boyhood. Mark Twain, who rose up out of the mid- and far-west, did much better at overcoming them.

As critical or offensive as Mark Twain may have been at times, he never wrote anything like what James wrote. The accusation of Twain's indulging in "anti-Semitic discourse" sits better upon his contemporary and fellow novelist and short-story writer, Henry James.

In the last year of his life Mark Twain had the opportunity to prove once more that he practiced what he preached about judging the individual, not whether he was gentile or Jew. His daughter Clara, had been a student of the pianist Theodor Leschetizky in Vienna in 1897–9. There she met a fellow student, about to begin a stellar career as a pianist and conductor, Ossip Gabrilowitsch, the son of Russian Jewish parents. The seeds of romance were planted. All the family were back in the United States ten years later, when, on October 6, 1909, Clara married him, "with the unreserved blessing of her father."[12] They were married by Mark's long-standing friend, the Protestant minister, Rev. Joseph Twitchell, and Twain, in regalia as a recipient of an Oxford University honorary degree, was photographed with the wedding party.[13] "I am glad of this marriage," he wrote to Mary Benjamin Rogers, "and Mrs. Clemens always had a warm affection for Gabrilowitsch."[14]

Father-in-law and son-in-law were close enough in affection that Ossip was sitting at his bedside during Twain's final moments. The *New York Times* reported that he asked him for his glasses to read further in Carlyle's *French Revolution.*[15] He died soon after. The Reverend Twitchell had the sad duty of conducting the funeral service for his famous friend Mark Twain two days after he died on April 21, 1910.

Gabrilowitsch deserves a paragraph on his own behalf. After a brilliant career as pianist and conductor of the Detroit and Philadelphia Symphonies, Ossip Gabrilowitsch died on September 14, 1936. He rated a column-long obituary in the *New York Times,* which did not fail to mention that he was the husband of the daughter of Mark Twain, dead now for more than a quarter-century. It also mentioned his defense of Arturo Toscanini against the Italian Fascists. This Jew's defense of the Italian conductor may remind one of his gentile father-in-law's defense of the Jew Dreyfus. The *Times* a day later devoted a brief editorial to him, emphasizing his contribution to American music and his sympathetic character. The editorial summed him up: "The artist was the man and the man was the artist," which would have delighted Twain, who judged each man on his own merits. The *Times* report of his funeral states that Ossip Gabrilowitsch was buried "at the foot of the body of Samuel L. Clemens" in the family plot in Woodlawn Cemetery, Elmira, New York.[16]

Mark Twain's last years concerning the Jews inspired Carl Dolmetsch to conclude:

> If any gentile may be called "philo-Semitic" in contradistinction to "anti-Semitic", it is Samuel L. Clemens, who, in both his public and private utterances and in the writings of Mark Twain, sedulously combated anti-Jewish prejudices.[17]

He had come a long way from the prejudices absorbed in the anti-Semitic atmosphere of Hannibal, Missouri to receive an accolade like this.

Chapter Eleven

AFTERWORD: DEFINING "ANTI-SEMITIC"

W E ARE TRAPPED by nomenclature and connotation. The single term "anti-Semitic" is universally applied to a multitude of gradations of this crime. For example, is the "anti-Semitic discourse" quoted in Andrea Greenbaum's article, "'A Number-One Troublemaker': Mark Twain's Anti-Semitic Discourse in Concerning the Jews" of the same nature as the "anti-Semitic discourse" in a characteristic diatribe in enormously popular 19th-century American missionary novels that harp on Jewish "blindness," "stiff-neckedness," money-obsession, where the author advocates conversion to Christianity as the only saving-grace available to the Jews?[1] Or, conditioned as we are to the cloud of the Holocaust of the 1940s hovering over us, is it fair, just, accurate, helpful to label Twain's "discourse" in the same category of Heinrich Himmler's anti-Semitic discourse to his SS troops to eradicate Jews? Obviously not, but we have no other terms to label these examples of discourse.

The connotation of "anti-Semitic" being so extremely amorphous, attempts have been made to coin a more exact differential terminology. Several suggestions have been offered: "anti-Jewish", or "Judeophobia," or decapitalizing "semitic," but all such attempts have come to failure, however. Sums up David Gerber, "In spite of its technical problems and the circumstances of its origin, 'Anti-Semitism' is still

widely employed in American literature and journalism, still sanc-
tioned by American dictionaries, and still expected by American
readers"[2] to cover all perceived instances of the phenomenon. Nevertheless, to arrive at a fair verdict in the debate about Mark Twain's
allusions, we need to define the nature of his anti-Semitic discourse
more particularly.

Luckily, Gerber has come to aid us. Like a legalist grading the
death of an individual all the way from involuntary homicide to first-
degree premeditated murder, Gerber has offered a pyramid of degrees
of "anti-Semitism" at least for Mark Twain's 19th-century American
democracy. Briefly stated, Gerber defines the term as a set of gradu-
ated beliefs that:

1. The Jewish race is "alien" in their creed, physiognomy, inner
nature, and psychology
2. Jews are money- and power-hungry, pushy, dishonest
3. The characteristics in 1 and 2 are not compensation for past persecution and victimization, but are signs of natural malevolence
toward others, especially non-Jews
4. Finally, the Jews must be denied social, legal equality and rights[3] –
"To put Jews in their place," as Jonathan Sarna says elsewhere.[4]

Gerber's definition is a dirge of degrees: Level 1 sees the race as being
different and apart, which in itself is not necessarily evil, only suspicious. In Level 2 suspicion has deepened into the anti-Semite's fear
that the Jewish race will not be satisfied with private difference only,
but will go public. Level 3 expresses the deeper fear that the Jewish
race will take action against their neighbors of other races, not as a
matter of revenge, but as an evil in their very nature. Thus far, these
levels focus on passive conditions and reactions on both Jewish and
anti-Jewish sides.

Finally, the fourth level switches from the evil of the Jews to ad-
vocacy of actions to control the racially uncontrollable. It is the cul-
mination of the anti-Semite's belief in the racial characteristics listed
on the lower levels of the definition. Level 4 begs us to ask judgmental

questions: What is the *motivation* behind given statements perceived to be "anti-Semitic"? Are they merely descriptive, fashionable, self-serving, uncomfortable, misguided, and essentially harmless? Or are they intended to be rousing, provocative, inciting action involving aggressive missionizing, social ostracism, legal restrictions, or physical attack on individuals and the race wherever found?

The danger of a naked use of the amorphous term "anti-semitic" is exemplified in the very title of Greenbaum's article. The term "anti-Semitic" seduced her into a making a dangerous insinuation in the "come-on" introductory phrase of the title. It implies that the phrase was written by Mark Twain and expresses his belief that the Jews are the "number-one" cause of "trouble" in the world, an accusation characteristically made by those who would exile, imprison, kill, or exterminate Jews. But her article nowhere gives an example in Mark Twain's works that he thought them to be trouble-makers. Indeed, he once pointed out, as we have noted, that it was Christians who operated in a bloodthirsty manner in the world, not the Jews. At the end of her essay she admits that Twain was not a "virulent anti-Semite," but that does not repair the implication she engendered by ripping the opening phrase of the title from a story by Bernard Malamud that, in a different genre altogether, had a different theme, locale, and purpose from those of Mark Twain. Yet, her problem was not only a choice of quotation, but of nomenclature: how else might one label discourse that slurs Jews?

I think we can agree that behind Mark Twain's early remarks there is no motivation to do any harm to any Jew, Jewish community, or the race at large. On the contrary, there is evidence that he abhorred such an attitude. Early on, in the *Alta California* letters, when the obnoxious "Isaac," representing for the moment the Jewish race, received his personal comeuppance, he metamorphosed in Twain's eyes into a defeated underdog, and it was his tormentors who became unsavory. From nearly the beginning of his journalistic career all the way through to its end, Twain employed his skill with satire to sympathize with Jewry – whether it was the distant Jewry of the Rhinelands in the era of the hypocritical crusades, or in a *fin de siecle* essay on the morality of the Spanish-American War. The Jews were simply victims, not the deservedly punished. These examples fall into Sarna's observation that anti-Semitism in 19th-century America displayed a dichotomy of mythical, stereotyped generalizations versus "the Jew next door," who is a good friend, neighbor, or associate.[5] Such, for Mark Twain, were Bret Harte for a while and Joe Goodman forever, and Daniel Frohman was simultaneously a stereotypical grasping Hebrew theatrical producer in civil court, but in the pool-parlor, he was a much-enjoyed adversary.

And, though he transformed the biblical Joseph from hero in *Innocents Abroad* to cruel monopolizer in "Concerning the Jews," Twain rejected out-of-hand the solution to the Jewish problem recommended by the Berlin lawyer – expulsion of the Jews. True, Jewish critics accused him of gross insensitivity and ignorance of the reality of the Jewish situation, yet not one suggested anything worse of him, all testifying to his goodwill. The ones presumably most sensitive and potentially most affected, the commonalty of Jews, saw no jot of anti-Semitism in him, and he felt no compunction in being in their midst. Yet, the term "anti-Semitism" dogged studies of Mark Twain's social attitudes.

So we are still faced with the semantic problem. How can we label Mark Twain's non-salutary remarks about Jews? Elsewhere in his essay on American anti-Semitism, Gerber proposes the tandem terms "ordinary," with which we may classify levels 1–3 of his definition vs. "extraordinary" anti-Semitism, which can describe level 4.[6] To relate these terms to Mark Twain's remarks, one would say that he is guilty of "ordinary" anti-Semitic utterances, not always discriminating between what is acceptable and what is a regurgitation of what Sarna called "a bad habit, imported from Europe."[7]

Other sub-terminologies describing the complexity of Mark Twain's judgments of his Jews are "ambivalence" and "parallel." The scholars whom I have invoked in this monograph all emphasize the "ambivalence" that Twain had regarding his Jews. Ambivalence is an uncomfortable term. Gerber defines "Ambivalence "[as the] gray areas between anti-Semitism and philo-Semitism."[8] "Ambivalence," to me, implies that there was a period of time that he saw the Jews negatively and then positively; or that one day, his views were left-of-center, the next day, right-of-center. Closer to semantic accuracy is Michael Dobkowski's statement: "Parallel sentiments were harbored by Mark Twain, who wavered between generous goodwill and latent prejudice, characteristic of the ambivalence of some of American opinion."[9] "Parallel" presumes an infinite separateness. It does not permit the turn to "philo-semitism" that a few critics awarded Mark Twain for his final writings.

A more preferable term might be *co-existence,* a more complicated mental phenomenon. *Co-existent* implies a living-together of feelings, a mutually tolerant, non-intrusive, never-accusative intertwining Frankly, I prefer an adjective more accurately defining Twain's attitude in the earlier phases of his career – *"innocent* anti-Semitic discourse." It is that innocence which spreads over the dichotomy – the ambivalence, if you prefer, or parallelism, or co-existence. In my estimation, even that ambiguous passage about a Jewish entity in Palestine wherein he suggests it would be best to curtail Jewish political power, is an instance of innocently misplaced humor.

As a summary generalization, then, recalling the Bible where Sam Clemens first met Mark Twain's Jews, I think it is fair and accurate to say that Mark Twain's words are sometimes the words of Esau, but the voice is always the voice of Jacob.

FACSIMILE OF "CONCERNING THE JEWS" BY MARK TWAIN

Harper's New Monthly Magazine,

September 1899

W MONTHLY MAGAZINE

SEPTEMBER, 1899   No. DXCII

CONCERNING THE JEWS.

BY MARK TWAIN.

SOME months ago I published a magazine article* descriptive of a remarkable scene in the Imperial Parliament in Vienna. Since then I have received from Jews in America several letters of inquiry. They were difficult letters to answer, for they were not very definite. But at last I have received a definite one. It is from a lawyer, and he really asks the questions which the other writers probably believed they were asking. By help of this text I will do the best I can to publicly answer this correspondent, and also the others—at the same time apologizing for having failed to reply privately. The lawyer's letter reads as follows:

I have read "Stirring Times in Austria." One point in particular is of vital import to not a few thousand people, including myself,

* See *Harper's Magazine* for March, 1898.

being a point about which I have often wanted to address a question to some disinterested person. The show of military force in the Austrian Parliament, which precipitated the riots, was not introduced by any Jew. No Jew was a member of that body. No Jewish question was involved in the Ausgleich or in the language proposition. No Jew was insulting anybody. In short, no Jew was doing any mischief toward anybody whatsoever. In fact, the Jews were the only ones of the nineteen different races in Austria which did not have a party—they are absolutely non-participants. Yet in your article you say that in the rioting which followed, all classes of people were unanimous only on one thing, viz., in being against the Jews. Now will you kindly tell me why, in your judgment, the Jews have thus ever been, and are even now, in these days of supposed intelligence, the butt of baseless, vicious animosities? I dare say that for centuries there has been no more quiet, undisturbing, and well-behaving citizens, as a class, than that same Jew. It seems to me that ignorance and fanaticism cannot alone account for these horrible and unjust persecutions.

Tell me, therefore, from your vantage-point of cold view, what in your mind is the cause. Can American Jews do anything to correct it either in America or abroad? Will it ever come to an end? Will a Jew be permitted to live honestly, decently, and peaceably like the rest of mankind? What has become of the golden rule?

·I will begin by saying that if I thought myself prejudiced against the Jew, I should hold it fairest to leave this subject to a person not crippled in that way. But I think I have no such prejudice. A few years ago a Jew observed to me that there was no uncourteous reference to his people in my books, and asked how it happened. It happened because the disposition was lacking. I am quite sure that (bar one) I have no race prejudices, and I think I have no color prejudices nor caste prejudices nor creed prejudices. Indeed, I know it. I can stand any society. All that I care to know is that a man is a human being—that is enough for me; he can't be any worse. I have no special regard for Satan; but I can at least claim that I have no prejudice against him. It may even be that I lean a little his way, on account of his not having a fair show. All religions issue bibles against him, and say the most injurious things about him, but we never hear *his* side. We have none but the evidence for the prosecution, and yet we have rendered the verdict. To my mind, this is irregular. It is un-English; it is un-American; it is French. Without this precedent Dreyfus could not have been condemned. Of course Satan has some kind of a case, it goes without saying. It may be a poor one, but that is nothing; that can be said about any of us. As soon as I can get at the facts I will undertake his rehabilitation myself, if I can find an unpolitic publisher. It is a thing which we ought to be willing to do for any one who is under a cloud. We may not pay him reverence, for that would be indiscreet, but we can at least respect his talents. A person who has for untold centuries maintained the imposing position of spiritual head of four-fifths of the human race, and political head of the whole of it, must be granted the possession of executive abilities of the loftiest order. In his large presence the other popes and

politicians shrink to midges for the microscope. I would like to see him. I would rather see him and shake him by the tail than any other member of the European Concert. In the present paper I shall allow myself to use the word Jew as if it stood for both religion and race. It is handy; and besides, that is what the term means to the general world.

In the above letter one notes these points:

1. The Jew is a well-behaved citizen.
2. Can ignorance and fanaticism *alone* account for his unjust treatment?
3. Can Jews do anything to improve the situation?
4. The Jews have no party; they are non-participants.
5. Will the persecution ever come to an end?
6. What has become of the golden rule?

Point No. 1.—We must grant proposition No. 1, for several sufficient reasons. The Jew is not a disturber of the peace of any country. Even his enemies will concede that. He is not a loafer, he is not a sot, he is not noisy, he is not a brawler nor a rioter, he is not quarrelsome. In the statistics of crime his presence is conspicuously rare—in all countries. With murder and other crimes of violence he has but little to do: he is a stranger to the hangman. In the police court's daily long roll of "assaults" and "drunk and disorderlies" his name seldom appears. That the Jewish home is a home in the truest sense is a fact which no one will dispute. The family is knitted together by the strongest affections; its members show each other every due respect; and reverence for the elders is an inviolate law of the house. The Jew is not a burden on the charities of the state nor of the city; these could cease from their functions without affecting him. When he is well enough, he works; when he is incapacitated, his own people take care of him. And not in a poor and stingy way, but with a fine and large benevolence. His race is entitled to be called the most benevolent of all the races of men. A Jewish beggar is not impossible, perhaps; such a thing may exist, but there are few men that can say they have seen that spectacle. The Jew has been staged in many uncomplimentary forms, but, so far as I know, no dramatist has done him the injustice to stage him as a beggar. Whenever a Jew has real need to beg, his people save him from the necessity of doing it. The charitable institutions of the Jews are supported by Jewish money, and amply. The Jews make no noise about it; it is done quietly; they do not nag and pester and harass us for contributions; they give us peace, and set us an example—an example which we have not found ourselves able to follow; for by nature we are not free givers, and have to be patiently and persistently hunted down in the interest of the unfortunate.

These facts are all on the credit side of the proposition that the Jew is a good and orderly citizen. Summed up, they certify that he is quiet, peaceable, industrious, unaddicted to high crimes and brutal dispositions; that his family life is commendable; that he is not a burden upon public charities; that he is not a beggar; that in benevolence he is above the reach of competition. These are the very quintessentials of good citizenship. If you can add that he is as honest as the average of his neighbors— But I think that question is affirmatively answered by the fact that he is a successful business man. The basis of successful business is honesty; a business cannot thrive where the parties to it cannot trust each other. In the matter of numbers the Jew counts for little in the overwhelming population of New York; but that his honesty counts for much is guaranteed by the fact that the immense wholesale business of Broadway, from the Battery to Union Square, is substantially in his hands.

I suppose that the most picturesque example in history of a trader's trust in his fellow-trader was one where it was not Christian trusting Christian, but Christian trusting Jew. That Hessian Duke who used to sell his subjects to George III. to fight George Washington with got rich at it; and by-and-by, when the wars engendered by the French Revolution made his throne too warm for him, he was obliged to fly the country. He was in a hurry, and had to leave his earnings behind—$9,000,000. He had to risk the money with some one without security. He did not select a Christian, but a Jew—a Jew of only modest means, but of high character; a character so high that it left him lonesome—Rothschild of Frankfort. Thirty years later, when Europe had become quiet and safe again, the Duke came back from overseas, and

the Jew returned the loan, with interest added.*

The Jew has his other side. He has some discreditable ways, though he has not a monopoly of them, because he cannot get entirely rid of vexatious Christian competition. We have seen that he seldom transgresses the laws against crimes of violence. Indeed, his dealings with courts are almost restricted to matters connected with commerce. He has a reputation for various small forms of cheating, and for practising oppressive usury, and for burning himself out to get the insurance, and for arranging cun-

* Here is another piece of picturesque history; and it reminds us that shabbiness and dishonesty are not the monopoly of any race or creed, but are merely human:

"Congress has passed a bill to pay $379 56 to Moses Pendergrass, of Libertyville, Missouri. The story of the reason of this liberality is pathetically interesting, and shows the sort of pickle that an honest man may get into who undertakes to do an honest job of work for Uncle Sam. In 1886 Moses Pendergrass put in a bid for the contract to carry the mail on the route from Knob Lick to Libertyville and Coffman, thirty miles a day, from July 1, 1887, for one year. He got the postmaster at Knob Lick to write the letter for him, and while Moses intended that his bid should be $400, his scribe carelessly made it $4. Moses got the contract, and did not find out about the mistake until the end of the first quarter, when he got his first pay. When he found at what rate he was working he was sorely cast down, and opened communication with the Post Office Department. The department informed him that he must either carry out his contract or throw it up, and that if he threw it up his bondsmen would have to pay the government $1459 85 damages. So Moses carried out his contract, walked thirty miles every week-day for a year, and carried the mail, and received for his labor $4—or, to be accurate, $6 84; for, the route being extended after his bid was accepted, the pay was proportionately increased. Now, after ten years, a bill was finally passed to pay to Moses the difference between what he earned in that unlucky year and what he received."

The *Sun*, which tells the above story, says that bills were introduced in three or four Congresses for Moses's relief, and that committees repeatedly investigated his claim.

It took six Congresses, containing in their persons the compressed virtues of 70,000,000 of people, and cautiously and carefully giving expression to those virtues in the fear of God and the next election, eleven years to find out some way to cheat a fellow-Christian out of about $13 on his honestly executed contract, and out of nearly $300 due him on its enlarged terms. And they succeeded. During the same time they paid out $1,000,000,000 in pensions—a third of it unearned and undeserved. This indicates a splendid all-around competency in theft, for it starts with farthings, and works its industries all the way up to ship-loads. It may be possible that the Jews can beat this, but the man that bets on it is taking chances.

ning contracts which leave him an exit but lock the other man in, and for smart evasions which find him safe and comfortable just within the strict letter of the law, when court and jury know very well that he has violated the spirit of it. He is a frequent and faithful and capable officer in the civil service, but he is charged with an unpatriotic disinclination to stand by the flag as a soldier—like the Christian Quaker.

Now if you offset these discreditable features by the creditable ones summarized in a preceding paragraph beginning with the words, "These facts are all on the credit side," and strike a balance, what must the verdict be? This, I think: that, the merits and demerits being fairly weighed and measured on both sides, the Christian can claim no superiority over the Jew in the matter of good citizenship.

Yet in all countries, from the dawn of history, the Jew has been persistently and implacably hated, and with frequency persecuted.

Point No. 2.—"Can fanaticism *alone* account for this?"

Years ago I used to think that it was responsible for nearly all of it, but latterly I have come to think that this was an error. Indeed, it is now my conviction that it is responsible for hardly any of it.

In this connection I call to mind Genesis, chapter xlvii.

We have all thoughtfully — or unthoughtfully—read the pathetic story of the years of plenty and the years of famine in Egypt, and how Joseph, with that opportunity, made a corner in broken hearts, and the crusts of the poor, and human liberty—a corner whereby he took a nation's money all away, to the last penny; took a nation's live-stock all away, to the last hoof; took a nation's land away, to the last acre; then took the nation itself, buying it for bread, man by man, woman by woman, child by child, till all were slaves; a corner which took everything, left nothing; a corner so stupendous that, by comparison with it, the most gigantic corners in subsequent history are but baby things, for it dealt in hundreds of millions of bushels, and its profits were reckonable by hundreds of millions of dollars, and it was a disaster so crushing that its effects have not wholly disappeared from Egypt to-day, more than three thousand years after the event.

Is it presumable that the eye of Egypt was upon Joseph the foreign Jew all this time? I think it likely. Was it friendly? We must doubt it. Was Joseph establishing a character for his race which would survive long in Egypt? and in time would his name come to be familiarly used to express that character—like Shylock's? It is hardly to be doubted. Let us remember that this was *centuries before the crucifixion.*

I wish to come down eighteen hundred years later and refer to a remark made by one of the Latin historians. I read it in a translation many years ago, and it comes back to me now with force. It was alluding to a time when people were still living who could have seen the Saviour in the flesh. Christianity was so new that the people of Rome had hardly heard of it, and had but confused notions of what it was. The substance of the remark was this: Some Christians were persecuted in Rome through error, they being "*mistaken for Jews.*"

The meaning seems plain. These pagans had nothing against Christians, but they were quite ready to persecute Jews. For some reason or other they hated a Jew before they even knew what a Christian was. May I not assume, then, that the persecution of Jews is a thing which *antedates* Christianity and was not born of Christianity? I think so. What was the origin of the feeling?

When I was a boy, in the back settlements of the Mississippi Valley, where a gracious and beautiful Sunday-school simplicity and unpracticality prevailed, the "Yankee" (citizen of the New England States) was hated with a splendid energy. But religion had nothing to do with it. In a trade, the Yankee was held to be about five times the match of the Westerner. His shrewdness, his insight, his judgment, his knowledge, his enterprise, and his formidable cleverness in applying these forces were frankly confessed, and most competently cursed.

In the cotton States, after the war, the simple and ignorant negroes made the crops for the white planter on shares. The Jew came down in force, set up shop on the plantation, supplied all the negro's wants on credit, and at the end of the season was proprietor of the negro's share of the present crop and of part of his share of the next one. Before long, the whites detested the Jew, and it is doubtful if the negro loved him.

The Jew is being legislated out of Russia. The reason is not concealed. The movement was instituted because the Christian peasant and villager stood no chance against his commercial abilities. He was always ready to lend money on a crop, and sell vodka and other necessaries of life on credit while the crop was growing. When settlement day came he owned the crop; and next year or year after he owned the farm, like Joseph.

In the dull and ignorant England of John's time everybody got into debt to the Jew. He gathered all lucrative enterprises into his hands; he was the king of commerce; he was ready to be helpful in all profitable ways; he even financed crusades for the rescue of the Sepulchre. To wipe out his account with the nation and restore business to its natural and incompetent channels he had to be banished the realm.

For the like reasons Spain had to banish him four hundred years ago, and Austria about a couple of centuries later.

In all the ages Christian Europe has been obliged to curtail his activities. If he entered upon a mechanical trade, the Christian had to retire from it. If he set up as a doctor, he was the best one, and he took the business. If he exploited agriculture, the other farmers had to get at something else. Since there was no way to successfully compete with him in any vocation, the law had to step in and save the Christian from the poorhouse. Trade after trade was taken away from the Jew by statute till practically none was left. He was forbidden to engage in agriculture; he was forbidden to practise law; he was forbidden to practise medicine, except among Jews; he was forbidden the handicrafts. Even the seats of learning and the schools of science had to be closed against this tremendous antagonist. Still, almost bereft of employments, he found ways to make money, even ways to get rich. Also ways to invest his takings well, for usury was not denied him. In the hard conditions suggested, the Jew without brains could not survive, and the Jew with brains had to keep them in good training and well sharpened up, or starve. Ages of restriction to the one tool which the law was not able to take from him—his brain— have made that tool singularly competent; ages of compulsory disuse of his hands have atrophied them, and he never

uses them now. This history has a very, very commercial look, a most sordid and practical commercial look, the business aspect of a Chinese cheap-labor crusade. Religious prejudices may account for one part of it, but not for the other nine.

Protestants have persecuted Catholics, but they did not take their livelihoods away from them. The Catholics have persecuted the Protestants with bloody and awful bitterness, but they never closed agriculture and the handicrafts against them. Why was that? That has the candid look of genuine religious persecution, not a trade-union boycott in a religious disguise.

The Jews are harried and obstructed in Austria and Germany, and lately in France; but England and America give them an open field and yet survive. Scotland offers them an unembarrassed field too, but there are not many takers. There are a few Jews in Glasgow, and one in Aberdeen; but that is because they can't earn enough to get away. The Scotch pay themselves that compliment, but it is authentic.

I feel convinced that the Crucifixion has not much to do with the world's attitude toward the Jew; that the reasons for it are older than that event, as suggested by Egypt's experience and by Rome's regret for having persecuted an unknown quantity called a Christian, under the mistaken impression that she was merely persecuting a Jew. *Merely* a Jew —a skinned eel who was used to it, presumably. I am persuaded that in Russia, Austria, and Germany nine-tenths of the hostility to the Jew comes from the average Christian's inability to compete successfully with the average Jew in business—in either straight business or the questionable sort.

In Berlin, a few years ago, I read a speech which frankly urged the expulsion of the Jews from Germany; and the agitator's *reason* was as frank as his proposition. It was this: *that eighty-five per cent. of the successful lawyers of Berlin were Jews, and that about the same percentage of the great and lucrative businesses of all sorts in Germany were in the hands of the Jewish race!* Isn't it an amazing confession? It was but another way of saying that in a population of 48,000,000, of whom only 500,000 were registered as Jews, eighty-five per cent. of the brains and honesty of the whole was lodged in the Jews. I must insist upon the honesty—it is an essential of successful business, taken by and large. Of course it does not rule out rascals entirely, even among Christians, but it is a good working rule, nevertheless. The speaker's figures may have been inexact, but *the motive of persecution* stands out as clear as day.

The man claimed that in Berlin the banks, the newspapers, the theatres, the great mercantile, shipping, mining, and manufacturing interests, the big army and city contracts, the tramways, and pretty much all other properties of high value, and *also* the small businesses— were in the hands of the Jews. He said the Jew was pushing the Christian to the wall all along the line; that it was all a Christian could do to scrape together a living; and that the Jew *must* be banished, and soon—there was no other way of saving the Christian. Here in Vienna, last autumn, an agitator said that all these disastrous details were true of Austria-Hungary also; and in fierce language he demanded the expulsion of the Jews. When politicians come out without a blush and read the baby act in this frank way, *unrebuked*, it is a very good indication that they have a market back of them, and know where to fish for votes.

You note the crucial point of the mentioned agitation; the argument is that the Christian cannot *compete* with the Jew, and that hence his very bread is in peril. To human beings this is a much more hate-inspiring thing than is any detail connected with religion. With most people, of a necessity, bread and meat take first rank, religion second. I am convinced that the persecution of the Jew is not due in any large degree to religious prejudice.

No, the Jew is a money-getter; and in getting his money he is a very serious obstruction to less capable neighbors who are on the same quest. I think that that is the trouble. In estimating worldly values the Jew is not shallow, but deep. With precocious wisdom he found out in the morning of time that some men worship rank, some worship heroes, some worship power, some worship God, and that over these ideals they dispute and cannot unite—but that they all worship money; so he made it the end and aim of his life to get it. He was at it in Egypt thirty-six centuries ago; he was at it in Rome when that Christian got persecuted by mistake for him; he has been at it ever since. The cost to him has been heavy; his success has made the whole human race his enemy—but it has paid, for it has brought him envy, and that is the only thing which men will sell both soul and body to get. He long ago observed that a millionaire commands respect, a two-millionaire homage, a multi-millionaire the deepest deeps of adoration. We all know that feeling; we have seen it express itself. We have noticed that when the average man mentions the name of a multi-millionaire he does it with that mixture in his voice of awe and reverence and lust which burns in a Frenchman's eye when it falls on another man's centime.

Point No. 4.—"The Jews have no party: they are non-participants."

Perhaps you have let the secret out and given yourself away. It seems hardly a credit to the race that it is able to say that; or to you, sir, that you can say it without remorse; more, that you should offer it as a plea against maltreatment, injustice, and oppression. Who gives the Jew the right, who gives any race the right, to sit still, in a free country, and let somebody else look after its safety? The oppressed Jew was entitled to all pity in the former times under brutal autocracies, for he was weak and friendless, and had no way to help his case. But he has ways now, and he has had them for a century, but I do not see that he has tried to make serious use of them. When the Revolution set him free in France it was an act of grace—the grace of other people; he does not appear in it as a helper. I do not know that he helped when England set him free. Among the Twelve Sane Men of France who have stepped forward with great Zola at their head to fight (and win, I hope and believe[*]) the battle for the most infamously misused Jew of modern times, do you find a great or rich or illustrious Jew helping? In the United States he was created free in the beginning—he did not need to help, of course. In Austria and Germany and France he has a vote, but of what considerable use is it to him? He doesn't seem to know how to apply it to the best effect. With all his

---

[*] The article was written in the summer of 1898. —ED.

splendid capacities and all his fat wealth he is to-day not politically important in any country. In America, as early as 1854, the ignorant Irish hod-carrier, who had a spirit of his own and a way of exposing it to the weather, made it apparent to all that he must be politically reckoned with; yet fifteen years before that we hardly knew what an Irishman looked like. As an intelligent force, and numerically, he has always been away down, but he has governed the country just the same. It was because he was *organized*. It made his vote valuable—in fact, essential.

You will say the Jew is everywhere numerically feeble. That is nothing to the point — with the Irishman's history for an object-lesson. But I am coming to your numerical feebleness presently. In all parliamentary countries you could no doubt elect Jews to the legislatures—and even *one* member in such a body is sometimes a force which counts. How deeply have you concerned yourselves about this in Austria, France, and Germany? Or even in America, for that matter? You remark that the Jews were not to blame for the riots in this Reichsrath here, and you add with satisfaction that there wasn't one in that body. That is not strictly correct; if it were, would it not be in order for you to explain it and apologize for it, not try to make a merit of it? But I think that the Jew was by no means in as large force there as he ought to have been, with his chances. Austria opens the suffrage to him on fairly liberal terms, and it must surely be his own fault that he is so much in the background politically.

As to your numerical weakness. I mentioned some figures awhile ago—500,000—as the Jewish population of Germany. I will add some more—6,000,000 in Russia, 5,000,000 in Austria, 250,000 in the United States. I take them from memory; I read them in the Cyclopædia Britannica ten or twelve years ago. Still, I am entirely sure of them. If those statistics are correct, my argument is not as strong as it ought to be as concerns America, but it still has strength. It is plenty strong enough as concerns Austria, for ten years ago 5,000,000 was nine per cent. of the empire's population. The Irish would govern the Kingdom of Heaven if they had a strength there like that.

I have some suspicions; I got them at second hand, but they have remained with me these ten or twelve years. When I read in the C. B. that the Jewish population of the United States was 250,000, I wrote the editor, and explained to him that I was personally acquainted with more Jews than that in my country, and that his figures were without a doubt a misprint for 25,000,000. I also added that I was personally acquainted with *that* many there; but that was only to raise his confidence in me, for it was not true. His answer miscarried, and I never got it; but I went around talking about the matter, and people told me they had reason to suspect that for business reasons many Jews whose dealings were mainly with the Christians did not report themselves as Jews in the census. It looked plausible; it looks plausible yet. Look at the city of New York; and look at Boston, and Philadelphia, and New Orleans, and Chicago, and Cincinnati, and San Francisco — how your race swarms in those places!—and everywhere else in America, down to the least little village. Read the signs on the marts of commerce and on the shops: Goldstein (gold stone), Edelstein (precious stone), Blumenthal (flower-vale), Rosenthal (rose-vale), Veilchenduft (violet odor), Singvogel (songbird), Rosenzweig (rose branch), and all the amazing list of beautiful and enviable names which Prussia and Austria glorified you with so long ago. It is another instance of Europe's coarse and cruel persecution of your race; not that it was coarse and cruel to outfit it with pretty and poetical names like those, but that it was coarse and cruel to make it *pay* for them or else take such hideous and often indecent names that to-day their owners never use them; or, if they do, only on official papers. And it was the many, not the few, who got the odious names, they being too poor to bribe the officials to grant them better ones.

Now why was the race renamed? I have been told that in Prussia it was given to using fictitious names, and often changing them, so as to beat the tax-gatherer, escape military service, and so on; and that finally the idea was hit upon of furnishing all the inmates of a house with *one and the same surname*, and then holding the house responsible right along for those inmates, and accountable for any disappearances that might occur; it made the Jews keep track of *each other*, for self-interest's sake, and saved the government the trouble.*

If that explanation of how the Jews of Prussia came to be renamed is correct, if it is true that they fictitiously registered themselves to gain certain advantages, it may possibly be true that in America they refrain from registering themselves as Jews to fend off the damaging prejudices of the Christian customer. I have no way of knowing whether this notion is well founded or not. There may be other and better ways of explaining why only that poor little 250,000 of our Jews got into the Cyclopædia. I may, of course, be mistaken, but I am strongly of the opinion that we have an immense Jewish population in America.

Point No. 3.—"Can Jews do anything to improve the situation?"

I think so. If I may make a suggestion without seeming to be trying to teach my grandmother how to suck eggs, I will offer it. In 'our days we have learned the value of combination. We apply it everywhere—in railway systems, in trusts, in trade unions, in Salvation Armies, in minor politics, in major politics, in European Concerts. Whatever our strength may be, big or little, we *organize* it. We have found out that that is the only way to get the most out of it that is in it. We know the weakness of individual sticks, and the strength of the concentrated fagot. Suppose you try a scheme like this, for instance. In England and America put every Jew on the census-book *as* a Jew (in case you have not been doing that). Get up volunteer regiments composed of Jews solely, and, when the drum beats, fall in and go to the front, so as to remove the reproach that you have few Massénas among you, and that you feed on a country but don't like to fight for it. Next, in politics, organize your strength, band together, and deliver the casting vote where you can, and where you can't, compel as good

terms as possible. You huddle to yourselves already in all countries, but you huddle to no sufficient purpose, politically speaking. You do not seem to be organized, except for your charities. There you are omnipotent; there you compel your due of recognition—you do not have to beg for it. It shows what you can do when you band together for a definite purpose.

And then from America and England you can encourage your race in Austria, France, and Germany, and materially help it. It was a pathetic tale that was told by a poor Jew in Galicia a fortnight ago during the riots, after he had been raided by the Christian peasantry and despoiled of everything he had. He said his vote was of no value to him, and he wished he could be excused from casting it, for indeed casting it was a sure *damage* to him, since no matter which party he voted for, the other party would come straight and take its revenge out of him. Nine per cent. of the population of the empire, these Jews, and apparently they cannot put a plank into any candidate's platform! If you will send our Irish lads over here I think they will organize your race and change the aspect of the Reichsrath.

You seem to think that the Jews take no hand in politics here, that they are "absolutely non-participants." I am assured by men competent to speak that this is a very large error, that the Jews are exceedingly active in politics all over the empire, but that they scatter their work and their votes among the numerous parties, and thus lose the advantages to be had by concentration. I think that in America they scatter too, but you know more about that than I do.

Speaking of concentration, Dr. Herzl has a clear insight into the value of that. Have you heard of his plan? He wishes to gather the Jews of the world together in Palestine, with a government of their own—under the suzerainty of the Sultan, I suppose. At the convention of Berne, last year, there were delegates from everywhere, and the proposal was received with decided favor. I am not the Sultan, and I am not objecting; but if that concentration of the cunningest brains in the world was going to be made in a free country (bar Scotland), I think it would be politic to stop it. It will not be well to let that race find out its strength. If the

---

* In Austria the renaming was merely done because the Jews in some newly acquired regions had no surnames, but were mostly named Abraham and Moses, and therefore the tax-gatherer could not tell t'other from which, and was likely to lose his reason over the matter. The renaming was put into the hands of the War Department, and a charming mess the graceless young lieutenants made of it. To them a Jew was of no sort of consequence, and they labelled the race in a way to make the angels weep. As an example, take these two: *Abraham Bellyache* and *Schmul Godbedamned.—Culled from* "*Namens Studien,*" *by Karl Emil Franzos.*

horses knew theirs, we should not ride any more.

Point No. 5.—"Will the persecution of the Jews ever come to an end?"

On the score of religion, I think it has already come to an end. On the score of race prejudice and trade, I have the idea that it will continue. That is, here and there in spots about the world, where a barbarous ignorance and a sort of mere animal civilization prevail; but I do not think that elsewhere the Jew need now stand in any fear of being robbed and raided. Among the high civilizations he seems to be very comfortably situated indeed, and to have more than his proportionate share of the prosperities going. It has that look in Vienna. I suppose the race prejudice cannot be removed; but he can stand that; it is no particular matter. By his make and ways he is substantially a foreigner wherever he may be, and even the angels dislike a foreigner. I am using this word foreigner in the German sense —*stranger*. Nearly all of us have an antipathy to a stranger, even of our own nationality. We pile gripsacks in a vacant seat to keep him from getting it; and a dog goes further, and does as a savage would—challenges him on the spot. The German dictionary seems to make no distinction between a stranger and a foreigner; in its view a stranger *is* a foreigner—a sound position, I think. You will always be by ways and habits and predilections substantially strangers—foreigners—wherever you are, and that will probably keep the race prejudice against you alive.

But you were the favorites of Heaven originally, and your manifold and unfair prosperities convince me that you have crowded back into that snug place again. Here is an incident that is significant. Last week in Vienna a hailstorm struck the prodigious Central Cemetery and made wasteful destruction there. In the Christian part of it, according to the official figures, 621 window-panes were broken; more than 900 singing-birds were killed; five great trees and many small ones were torn to shreds and the shreds scattered far and wide by the wind; the ornamental plants and other decorations of the graves were ruined, and more than a hundred tomb-lanterns shattered; and it took the cemetery's whole force of 300 laborers more than three days to clear away the storm's wreckage. In

the report occurs this remark—and in its italics you can hear it grit its Christian teeth: ".... lediglich die *israelitische* Abtheilung des Friedhofes vom Hagelwetter *gänzlich verschont* worden war." Not a hailstone hit the Jewish reservation! Such nepotism makes me tired.

Point No. 6.—"What has become of the golden rule?"

It exists, it continues to sparkle, and is well taken care of. It is Exhibit A in the Church's assets, and we pull it out every Sunday and give it an airing. But you are not permitted to try to smuggle it into this discussion, where it is irrelevant and would not feel at home. It is strictly religious furniture, like an acolyte, or a contribution-plate, or any of those things. It has never been intruded into business; and Jewish persecution is not a religious passion, it is a business passion.

To conclude.—If the statistics are right, the Jews constitute but *one per cent.* of the human race. It suggests a nebulous dim puff of star dust lost in the blaze of the Milky Way. Properly the Jew ought hardly to be heard of; but he is heard of, has always been heard of. He is as prominent on the planet as any other people, and his commercial importance is extravagantly out of proportion to the smallness of his bulk. His contributions to the world's list of great names in literature, science, art, music, finance, medicine, and abstruse learning are also away out of proportion to the weakness of his numbers. He has made a marvellous fight in this world, in all the ages; and has done it with his hands tied behind him. He could be vain of himself, and be excused for it. The Egyptian, the Babylonian, and the Persian rose, filled the planet with sound and splendor, then faded to dream-stuff and passed away; the Greek and the Roman followed, and made a vast noise, and they are gone; other peoples have sprung up and held their torch high for a time, but it burned out, and they sit in twilight now, or have vanished. The Jew saw them all, beat them all, and is now what he always was, exhibiting no decadence, no infirmities of age, no weakening of his parts, no slowing of his energies, no dulling of his alert and aggressive mind. All things are mortal but the Jew; all other forces pass, but he remains. What is the secret of his immortality?

131.

ABBREVIATIONS AND BIBLIOGRAPHY
OF WORKS CONSULTED

Abbreviations precede standard bibliographical data. The intention of this procedure is to cite all references in the Notes only by abbreviations or author, or author + short form of the title. Thus the reader has the convenience of looking up the full bibliographical data easily in the listing below.

[*Alta Cal.*] *Alta California* (San Francisco newspaper), February and March, 1867. Website: www.twainquote.com. Link: "Newspaper Articles"

["CJ"] "Concerning the Jews," in Neider ed. (q.v)

[*EJ*] *Encyclopedia Judaica* (Keter, Jerusalem, 1972)

[*Inn Abr*] Mark Twain, *The Innocents Abroad* (1869; New York, Book-of-the-Month Club, 1992). Two facsimile volumes in one.

[*MTA*] Mark Twain, *The Autobiography of Mark Twain,* ed. Charles Neider, New York, Harper, 1959

[*MTA-Z*] *Mark Twain A–Z.* Rasmussen, R. Kent ed. New York, Oxford U P, 1996

[*MTCR*] *Mark Twain's Correspondence with Henry Huttleston Rogers.* Lewis Leary ed. U of California P, 1969

[*MTEncyc*] *Mark Twain Encyclopedia*. Ed. J.R. Lemaster and James D. Wilson. New York / London, 1993

[MTH] *Mark Twain-Howells Letters: Correspondence of Samuel L. Clemens and William Dean Howells, 1872–1910*. Cambridge, Harvard U P, 1960

[MTL] *Mark Twain's Letters*. Ed. Victor Fischer *et al.* Berkeley, U of California P, 1995

[MTN] *Mark Twain's Notebooks and Journals. Vol. 1 (1855–73)*. Ed. Frederick Anderson *et al.* Berkeley, U of California P, 1975

American Hebrew (New York weekly magazine).

Andriano, Joseph. "Extract from Captain Stormfield's Visit to Heaven." *MTEncyc*, 272

Appel, John J. "Mark Twain's View of Jews." *Congress Weekly*, December 6, 1954, 16–18.

Baetzhold, Howard G. "'Word of Encouragement for our Blushing Exiles.'" *MTEncyc*, 798–9

BenArieh, Yehoshua. *Jerusalem in the 19th Century: The Old City*. Jerusalem, The Ben Zvi Institute, New York, St. Martin's: Press, 1984

Berkove, Lawrence. "Goodman, Joseph Thompson.' *Dictionary of National Biography*, IX: 244–6

Briden, Earl. "Dueling." *MTEncyc*, 233–4

Davis, Helen I. "Bret Harte and his Jewish Ancestor, Bernard Hart." *Publications of the American Historical Society*, 32 (1931), 99–111

DeVoto, Bernard. "Mark Twain About the Jews." *Jewish Frontier*, 6 (May 1939), 7–9

—— ed. *The Portable Mark Twain*. New York, Viking, 1946

Dobkowski, Michael. *The Tarnished Dream: The Basis of American Anti-Semitism*. Westport, Conn., Greenwood, 1979

Dolmetsch, Carl. "Freud, Sigmund." *MTEncyc*, 308–9

—— "Jews" *MTEncyc*, 413–5

—— "Mark Twain and the Viennese Anti-Semites: New Light on 'Concerning the Jews.'" *Mark Twain Journal*, 23:2 (Fall 1985), 10–17

———'Our Famous Guest': *Mark Twain in Vienna*. Athens, Georgia, U of Georgia P, 1992

Duckett, Margaret. *Mark Twain and Bret Harte*. Norman, U of Oklahoma P, 1964

Encyclopedia Britannica. 15th ed. (1985) vol IV:

Ensor, Allison. *Mark Twain and the Bible*. Lexington, U of Kentucky P, 1969

Feldman, Egal. *The Dreyfus Affair and the American Conscience*. Detroit, Wayne State U P, 1981

Fishkin, Shelley. "Racial Attitudes." *MTEncyc*, 609–14

Foner, Philip. *Mark Twain: Social Critic*. New York, International Publishers, 1958

Freud, Sigmund. "A Comment on Anti-Semitism." *Complete Psychological Works of Sigmund Freud*, trans. James Shackey *et al*. London, Hogarth, 1964

Gerber, David A. "Anti-Semitism and Jewish-Gentile Relations in American Historiography and the American Past." In David Gerber, ed. *Anti-Semitism in American History*. Urbana, U of Illinois P, 1986

Gibson, William. *Mark Twain's Mysterious Stranger Manuscripts*. Berkeley, U of California P, 1969

Gillman, Susan. "Mark Twain's Travels in the Racial Occult: *Following the Equator* and the Dream Tales." *Cambridge Companion to Mark Twain*, ed. Forrest G. Robinson. Cambridge U P, 1995

Gilman, Sander L. "Mark Twain and the Diseases of the Jews." *American Literature* 65 (March 1993), 95–115

Greenbaum, Andrea. "'A Number-One Troublemaker': Mark Twain's Anti-Semitic Discourse in 'Concerning the Jews.'" *Studies in American-Jewish Literature* 15(1996), 73–7

Gribben, Alan. *Mark Twain's Library: A Reconstruction*. Boston, G.K. Hall, 1980

Harap, Louis. *The Image of the Jew in American Literature*. Philadelphia, Jewish Publication Society, 1974

Herzl, Theodor. *Diaries*. trans. Marvin Lowenthal. London, Gollancz, 1956

————"Mark Twain and the British Ladies," trans. Alfred Werner. *Commentary* XXVII (September 1959), 243–5

————"Mark Twain in Paris" trans. Alexander Behn. *Mark Twain Quarterly* IX (Winter 1951), 16–20 The German original *feuilleton* carried the same title as this translation.

Howe, Irving and Ruth Wisse. *The Best of Sholom Aleichem.* New York: Touchstone Press, 1979

James, Henry. *The American Scene.* Introd. Irving Howe. New York: Horizon, 1967

Kahn, Sholom J. *Mark Twain's Mysterious Stranger: A Study of the Manuscript Texts.* Columbia, U of Missouri P, 1978

————"Mark Twain's Philo-Semitism: 'Concerning the Jews.'" *Mark Twain Journal* 23:2 (Fall 1985), 18–26

Kaplan, Justin. *Mr. Clemens and Mark Twain.* New York: Simon and Schuster, 1966

Leary, Lewis ed. *Mark Twain's Letters to Mary.* New York, Columbia U P, 1961

Leviant, Curt. "Introduction." *Some Laughter, Some Tears.* (Stories by Sholom Aleichem) New York, Putnam Paragon Books, 1968

Lynn, Kenneth S. *Mark Twain and Southwestern Humor.* Boston, Little-Brown, 1959

Neider, Charles ed. *The Complete Essays of Mark Twain.* Garden City, Doubleday, 1963

————ed. *The Complete Humorous Sketches and Tales of Mark Twain.* Garden City, Hanover House, 1961

————ed. *The Complete Short Stories of Mark Twain.* New York, Bantam pb, 1981

New York Times. October 20, 22, 1906

Nixon, Jude, "Social Philosophy," *MTEncyc,* 694–7

Ozick, Cynthia. "Mark Twain and the Jews. *Commentary,* May, 1995, 56–62

Pattee, Fred L. ed. *Mark Twain: Representative Selections.* New York, American Book Co., 1935

Postal, Bernard and Lionel Koppman. *A Jewish Tourist's Guide to the U.S.* Philadelphia, Jewish Publication, Society, 1954

Richmond, Marian A. "The Lost Source in Freud's 'Comment on Anti-Semitism': Mark Twain." *Journal of the American Psychoanalytic Association* 28 (1980), 563–74

Rourke, Constance. *American Humor: A Study of the National Character.* 1931; New York, Harcourt, Brace, 1959

Sarna, Jonathan. "The Mythical Jew and the Jew Next Door in the 19th Century." In David Gerber, ed. *Anti-Semitism in American History.* Urbana, Ill.: U of Illinois P, 1986

Schoffman, Stuart. "Russian Rhapsody." *Eretz* magazine (Israel) 80 (February 2002). 1950

Skandera, Laura E. "Gabrilowitsch, Ossip." *MTEncyc,* 312

Smith, Janet ed. *Mark Twain on the Damned Human Race.* New York, Hill and Wang, 1962

Stewart, H.L. "Mark Twain on the Jewish Problem." *Dalhousie Review* 14 (January 1935), 455–8

Tuckey, John S. *Mark Twain's "Fables of Man."* Berkeley, U of California P, 1972

Mark Twain's The Mysterious Stranger and the Critics. Belmont, Cal., Wadsworth, 1968

Vogel, Dan. "Concerning Mark Twain's Jews." *Studies in American Jewish Literature* 12 (1998) 152–5

Waife-Goldberg, Marie. *My Father, Sholom Aleichem.* New York, Schocken pb. 1971

Whicher. Stephen ed. *Selections from Ralph Waldo Emerson.* Boston, Houghton-Mifflin pb, 1957

NOTES

1: "THE HANNIBAL SYNDROME".

1. *MTA-Z*, "Chronology", x.
2. Harap, 349.
3. Dolmetsch, *MTEncyc*, 413.
4. *MTA*, 77.
5. Foner, 222.
6. Foner, 222.
7. Gillman, 210.
8. Dolmetsch, *Vienna*, 287.
9. De Voto, *Portable MT*, 632.
10. Harap, 47–64, *passim;* see also Garber, 22: "Negative religious and social stereotypes and images were quite common.".
11. Foner, 222.
12. Smith, 159.
13. Smith, 159.
14. Foner, 222–3.
15. Neider ed., *Essays, 18.*
16. Neider ed., *Essays,* 447; for dating, see Neider's note, *Essays,* 452.
17. Dolmetsch, *Vienna,* 217.

2: OUT WEST WITH TWO JEWS AND A RIGHTEOUS GENTILE.

1. Postal/Koppman, 294.
2. Postal/Koppman, 294, 298. Harap, p. 71, remarks that there was little intolerance in the Far West.
3. Neider ed., *Humorous Sketches,* 186–8.
4. Rourke, 167–8.
5. Rourke, 175; see also Lynn, 148.
6. Neider ed., "Note on 'The Petrified Man,'" *Humorous Sketches,* 149.

7. *MTA-Z*, 504.
8. Kaplan, 36.
9. Davis, 104.
10. Davis, 104.
11. Davis, 105; note 15.
12. Harap, 344.
13. Kaplan, 73.
14. Kaplan, 32, 74, 72.
15. Kaplan, 107.
16. Kaplan, 107.
17. Kaplan, 107.
18. Kaplan, 129–31 passim.
19. DeVoto ed., *Portable MT*, 745.
20. Kaplan, 150.
21. Kaplan, 201.
22. Kaplan, 199.
23. Kaplan 204.
24. Kaplan, 334.
25. DeVoto ed., *Portable MT*, 752.
26. See Duckett, 172 ff.
27. Harap, 345.
28. Kaplan, 355.
29. Neider ed., *Essays*, 430–1.
30. Postal/Koppman, 298.
31. Postal/Koppman, 54, 42, 65.
32. The only source that I have come across that says that Joseph Thompson Goodman, editor of the Virginia City *Territorial Enterprise*, was Jewish is the *Jewish Tourist's Guide*, which has been taken as accurate by the *Encyclopedia Judaica* (12:1016–17). Unfortunately, *The Tourist's Guide* does not have citations of sources. The biographical sketch in *Dictionary of National Biography* has not a word about any kind of Jewish connection. My further internet researches at the Mark Twain Project at Berkeley yielded photostats of documents relating to the transfer of the remains of Goodman's parents from one cemetery to another. One photostat did mention the name of a rabbi in San Diego who had provided "information." He replied to my query to him with the comment that he knew nothing about Joseph's ancestry. He did not elaborate on the strange fact that he provided information to the authorities transferring the remains. That the rabbi's name appears on the document may be sufficient to indicate that Goodman was somehow Jewish.
33. Dolmetsch, "Jews." *MTEncyc*, 413.
34. Harap, 280. Harap gives an excellent synopsis of her Jewishness on pages 279–83.
35. *EJ* 11:cols 1353–4.

36. Postal/Koppman, 295.
37. Postal/Koppman, 295; MTA-Z, under "Menken.".
38. Kaplan, 46.
39. Kaplan, 136.
40. Berkove, 245.
41. Kaplan, 169.
42. Postal / Koppman, 298.

3. "ISAAC" THE TERRIBLE.

1. Kaplan, 16–17.
2. The synopsis here combines elements from Twain's Notebook #7, 1:253 ff, and the account in the letter of Dec. 23, 1866, published in the *Alta California*, Feb. 24, 1867,.
3. To clarify the mis-chronolgy here: the notes in *Notebook #7*, 1:260 ff. are largely undated; the letter published on Feb. 24. carries the date Dec. 23; the one published on Feb. 27 is dated Dec. 20; the March 15 publication is the letter Twain had dated "Christmas Eve" and "Christmas night."
4. *Alta Cal.*, Feb. 27, 1867.
5. *Alta Cal.*, Mar. 15, 1867.
6. Notebook #7, p. 267; see note 33, p. 266.
7. *Alta Cal.*, March 15, 1867.
8. Harap, 352.

4. THE NOT-SO-INNOCENTS ABROAD.

1. *Inn. Abr.*, 40. Subsequent page references to *Innocents Abroad* will be inserted in parentheses.
2. Just a few years earlier, in 1864, Twain wrote a sketch in which he satirized the climate of Nevada: after a few days of rain in November, "you may loan out your umbrella for twelve months, with the serene confidence which a Christian feels in four aces" ("Information for the Million," Neider ed, *Humorous Sketches*, 32). Is he satirizing Christianity, or Christians out of anti-Christian prejudice? I think not. Mark Twain is simply being innocently irreverently humorous.
3. Gilman, 103.
4. Ensor, 6, 24, 91 ff.
5. Gilman, 96–7.
6. Gilman, 97.
7. Greenbaum, 73.
8. Dolmetsch, "Viennese Anti-Semites," 17, note 16.
9. See Gribben, *passim*.
10. Ben Arieh, 275, 321, 322.
11. Neider ed., *Essays*, 101.
12. Kaplan, 20–1.
14. Lynn, 151.

5: A 30-YEARS' MISCELLANY.

1. Pattee, 98.
2. Harap, 438.
3. Kaplan, 95–6.
4. Kahn, 18–19.
5. Foner, 225.
6. Mark Twain, *Life on the Mississippi*, 290–1.
7. It was Adjutant C.E.S. Wood, of West Point, inquiring on behalf of a Jewish friend of his. *MTH*, 555.
8. Kahn, 19.
9. Nieder ed., *Essays*. 576 It was first published posthumously in 1923 (p. 583).
10. Whicher ed., 153.
11. Neider ed., *Essays*, 578.
12. Neider ed., *Essays*, 583.
13. Neider ed., *Essays*, 526–7.
14. Neider, *Essays*, 583.
15. *MTH*, 560.
16. *MTCR*, 242.
17. *MTCR*, 238n.
18. *MTCR*, 325.
19. *MTCR*, 349.
20. Harap, 6–7.
21. Sarna, 66.
22. Gerber, 19.
23. Kaplan, 323.

6. A TRIAD OF EUROPEAN JEWS.

1. Kahn, 21; Feldman, 8.
2. Harap, 355, from a previously unpublished letter.
3. Neider ed., *Humorous Sketches*, 673.
4. Neider ed., *Humorous Sketches*, 678.
5. Neider, *Humorous Sketches*, 662 ff. Dating this essay as 1898 (Neider, 671, Chronology in *MTA-Z*) is questionable, because the Dreyfus retrial verdict was handed down in September 1899 (*EJ*, 6:228). See also Dolmetsch, *Vienna*, 173.
6. Dolmetsch, *Vienna*, 320.
7. *Mark Twain Quarterly* 9 (Winter 1951), 16–20. Alfred Werner published a different translation, under the title "Mark Twain and the British Ladies: *Commentary* 27 (September 1959), 243–5.
8. Herzl, *Diaries*, 114.
9. Dolmetsch, "Anti-Semitism in Vienna," 12.
10. Dolmetsch, *Vienna*, 42–3.
11. Dolmetsch, *Vienna*, 129.
12. Dolmetsch, 270.

13. Dolmetsch, *Vienna,* 266.
14. Dolmetsch, *Vienna,* 268–9.
15. Dolmetsch, *Vienna,* 136.
16. Dolmetsch, *MTEncy,* 308.
17. Dolmetsch, *Vienna,* 2,4.

7. SHOCK TREATMENT IN VIENNA.

1. Dolmetsch, 166 ff.
2. Kaplan, 215; Dolmetsch, *Vienna,* 11, 40 ff.
3. Dolmetsch, *Vienna,* 34.
4. Qu. Dolmetsch, "Anti-Semitism in Vienna," 10.
5. Smith, 158.
6. Dolmetsch, *Vienna,* 42, 165.
7. Dolmetsch, *Vienna,* 45.
8. Dolmetsch, *Vienna,* 72.
9. Neider ed., *Essays,* 211 ff. The facts reported in the present paragraphs are culled from Twain's essay, not from an authoritative history of the Empire.
10. Neider ed., *Essays,* 223.
11. Neider ed., *Essays,* 223.
12. Neider ed., *Essays,* 227, trans. in a note. Twain's italics and square brackets.
13. Neider ed., *Essays,* 234–5.
14. Pawel, 60. *New Yorker* magazine, January 11, 1999, 82.

8. CONCERNING "CONCERNING THE JEWS".

1. Tuckey, "Fables," 445. Paraphrases and quotation from the letter will be cited in my text.
2. Dolmetsch, *Vienna,* 164. *The American Hebrew* published whatever answers it received on April 4, 1890. Harap, 88 ff., and Dobkowski, 98, synopsize several answers.
3. Qu. Dolmetsch, "Anti-S in Vienna," 10; see also, p. 14.
4. Dolmetsch, *Vienna,* 174.
5. Neider ed., "Concerning the Jews," *Essays,* 163. Page references to this essay will be given in parentheses with the rubric "CJ". See also Smith's introduction to the text of the essay, 161.
6. Smith,157.
7. On this point see Harap, 352–4 passim, and Ozick, "Mark Twain and the Jews," 61.
8. Gilman, 112.
9. Kaplan, 116.
10. Neider ed., *Essays,* 174.
11. Stewart, 455–8 passim.
12. James Bryce, "Lord Beaconsfield," *Century,* 23 (March 1882), 729–44; Emma Lazarus, "Was the Earl of Beaconsfield a Representative Jew?", *Century,* 23

(April 1882), 939–42. For a fuller discussion of the *Century* debate see my *Emma Lazarus* (Boston, Twayne's USAS 353, 1980), 136–9 For Twain's connection to *Century* in those years, see Kaplan, 263.

13. Stewart, 456.
14. Dolmetsch, *Vienna,* 172.
15. Dolmetsch, *MTEncyc,* under "Jews," 413.
16. Gilman, 108.
17. Stuart Schoffman "Russian Rhapsody", *Eretz* magazine (Israel), 8 (Feb 2000), 39.
18. MTCR, 354.
19. MTCR, 354.
20. MTCR, 372; for the amount of the fee, see p. 354, note 1.
21. Neider ed, *Essays,* xxii.
22. Harap, 356.
23. Foner, 233.
24. *American Hebrew,* October 6, p. 677.
25. Dolmetsch, *MTEncyc,* 415.
26. Stewart, 456.
27. DeVoto 7,9. Dolmetsch labels Edmonson as "an American Nazi." *Vienna,* 178.
28. Appel, 18.
29. Nixon, "Social Philosophy," *MTEncyc,* 696.
30. Ozick, 61.

9. TWO FANTASIES AND A TWICE-TOLD TALE.
1. *Notebooks,* 1:241.
2. Smith, 178.
3. Smith, 178.
4. Neider, *Essays,* 18.
5. Neider, *Essays,* 447.
6. *MTEncyc,* 415.
7. Smith, 159.
8. Harap, 351.
9. Gibson, 473.
10. Stucky, *Mysterious Stranger and the Critics,* 90.
11. Gibson, 5; see also the Appendix of textual emendations.
12. Gibson, 43.
13. Gibson, 59.
14. Gibson, 162.
15. Gibson, 473.
16. Dolmetsch, *Vienna,* 292.
17. Gillman 213 and 211, where she quotes Twain's autobiography.
18. Lynn, 280–1; see also, p. 243.

19. Dolmetsch, *Vienna,* 287; Gillman, 211.

20. Gillman, 210.

21. Gibson, 379.

22. Kahn, *Manuscripts,* 170.

23. Tuckey, *Fables,* 279–289; references to specific pages will be enclosed in parentheses.

24. Lynn, 280–1.

25. Harap, 352.

26. Dolmetsch, *Vienna,* 164.

27. Briden, 234.

28. Fishkin, 613.

10. ADULATION AT THE END.

1. Foner, 236.

2. Smith, 158.

3. Foner, 236.

4. MTA-Z, Chronology, xxiii.

5. Harap 390–1.

6. Leviant, Introduction, 17, Waife-Goldberg did not list the 1918 translation in her "Works of Sholom Aleichem in English Translation," in *My Father, Sholom Aleichem,* 318–19.

7. The October 20th item appears on page 5, that of Oct. 22nd on page 7 of the *Times.*

8. Waife-Goldberg, 187.

9. Harap 357, citing Caroline Harnsburger, *Mark Twain: Family Man* (1960).

10. James, 131 (Further page references in parentheses).

11. For Louis Harap's discussion of James's *American Scene,* see Harap, 375–6. I think Harap is too kind.

12. Dolmetsch, *MTEncyc,* 415.

13. Kaplan, 387. The photograph is reproduced in MTA-Z, 161.

14. Leary, "*Letters to Mary,*" 127–8.

15. Skandera, *MTEncyc,* 312; *New York Times,* April 22, 1910 (p. 1, col. 1).

16. *EJ,* 12: 690; *New York Times,* Sept 15, 16, Sept. 18, 1936.

17. Dolmetsch, *MTEncyc,* 413.

10. AFTERWORD: DEFINING "ANTI-SEMITIC".

1. See Harap' survey, chaps. 7 and 8.

2. Gerber 39, note 1.

3. Gerber, 3.

4. Sarna, 67.

5. Sarna, 58.

6. Gerber, 22, 29. The terminology is Gerber's; relationship to his definition is mine.
7. Qu. by Gerber, 9.
8. Gerber, 7.
9. Dobkowski, 98.

INDEX

Pseudonyms are found under the familiar form of the pseudonym, e.g., Artemus Ward, Mark Twain. References to "Mark Twain", "Twain," "Sam Clemens," "Samuel Langhorne Clemens" all appear under Mark Twain; other members of the Clemens family, are individuated under Clemens.